Josef Frank – Spaces

Mikael Bergquist & Olof Michélsen

PARK BOOKS

SPACES

INTRODUCTION
The Little Big House. On Frank's Villas
7

CASE STUDY 1
Claëson House, Falsterbo, 1924–1927
22

CASE STUDY 2
House for Vienna XIII, 1926
40

CASE STUDY 3
House for M S, Los Angeles, 1930
52

CASE STUDY 4
Villa Beer, Vienna, 1930
64

CASE STUDY 5
Villa Wehtje, Falsterbo, 1936
80

CASE STUDY 6
Accidental House, Fantasy House no. 9, 1947
98

TIMELINE
Josef Frank Villas, 1913–1957
114

The Little Big House.
On Frank's Villas

Introduction by Mikael Bergquist and Olof Michélsen

Josef Frank is both a complicated architect and a simple one. Frank's colleague Ernst A. Plischke described him as an intellectual engaged in architecture, not an intellectual architect. There is a deceptive ease in Frank's drawing mannerisms and airy perspective sketches—an inviting atmosphere that can seduce the viewer into not immediately understanding the multiple layers in Frank's architecture. Josef Frank advocates a freedom where the user is permitted to have their bad taste and inherited furniture. It is a critique of the *Gesamtkunstwerk*

Josef Frank 1885–1967.

and the architect who wants aesthetic control over everything. However, this does not mean the architect's role should be passive, but instead, an approach where the architecture is kept in the background and where the refined and the banal are combined. In his book on photography, Roland Barthes uses the concept of *punctum*.[1] It represents a small detail that stands out and catches the viewer's attention. The same kind of concentration is found in Frank's houses. Whilst the architecture does not speak with grand gestures, there is an almost "equilibristic" manner to the design of individual components and details like stairs, handrails, furniture, and fireplaces.

A fundamental quality in Frank's architecture is scale. The size of the project has no significance in this context. From the smallest house to the largest, one finds the same type of spatial qualities. Frank was very aware of how small dimensional changes can be crucial in architecture. Room heights, the size and placement of windows, and the way daylight guides us through a building.

Certainty of measurements also applies to Frank's furniture. They exhibit concentration and playful elegance. From the mid-1920s, he developed different types of chairs and furniture in long series of variations with small dimensional changes, down to single centimeters.[2]

Our starting point for this work was to undertake an analysis and architectural examination of Frank's residential houses. What are the special qualities of these houses? How is the circulation formed? How are open spaces placed against closed ones? How does the interior relate to the exterior? How did he work with form and volume? How did he use repetitive elements such as staircases? And numerous other questions.

Our work is not primarily a historical study; we believe that Frank's work process and methods are still relevant and useful for us as practicing architects today. We have selected and

Interior from Frank's double house at the Weißenhofsiedlung, 1927.

studied six of Frank's villas. We have chosen these houses as they illustrate different aspects of Frank's rich work. Some of them are large and have been realized, such as Villa Beer in Vienna and Villa Wehtje in Falsterbo in southern Sweden; others are unrealized projects such as the House for M S and Fantasy House no. 9. In addition, others show aspects of intricate spatial puzzles, such as House for Vienna XIII.

In the summer of 1927, the Weißenhofsiedlung housing exhibition in Stuttgart was inaugurated. The only Austrian architect invited by Mies van der Rohe to participate was Josef Frank. He contributed a semi-detached two-family house, not significantly different from the outside from the other buildings in the exhibition. It had stucco façades, a flat roof, horizontal windows, and large glazed openings. But instead

Josef Frank's living room at the exhibition at Liljevalchs Konsthall, 1934.

of tubular-steel furniture, which was the standard in the other interiors, Frank furnished his house with furniture from his own interior firm Haus & Garten: overstuffed lounge chairs, cretonnes with strong colorful patterns, ceiling-to-floor curtains, carpets, sofas with pillows, and brass lighting fixtures with sewn lampshades. Frank was criticized for his feminine interiors. The project was referred to as "Frank's brothel."[3] In his text in the exhibition catalog Frank wrote: "One can use everything that can be used."[4]

By the end of 1933, Frank left Vienna for Sweden with his Swedish wife Anna. There, the first presentation of his work in public appeared at the exhibition called *Vackrare vardagsvara* [Attractive articles for everyday use] at Liljevalchs Konsthall, organized by the Swedish Society of Crafts and Design in summer 1934. Frank had already been affiliated with the interior firm Svenskt Tenn in Stockholm at the time. His interior room features were very different from all the other exhibitors' designs. In his suite of rooms, the living room aroused the greatest attention. An oversized sofa clad in a flower-patterned Baker cretonne dominated the room. The sofa was intended for lying down rather than sitting on: its large depth made comfortable sitting almost impossible. On the wall was a ceiling-high mirror, in the front corner of the room an open cocktail cabinet, and on the floor in front of the cabinet a leopard skin. The room's decadent atmosphere could not have been more foreign to the sober, rational Welfare Society interiors that surrounded it.

It is possible to see Josef Frank's attitude in the two examples above as purely provocative—and that is certainly true in some ways—but more than anything it was an expression of a deeply rooted skepticism towards all-embracing systems, towards the belief in a ruling style, and towards a one-dimensional view of life. It was also a conscious statement against the regimentation in early modernism's puritanical interiors and the desire for consistency of house and furniture.

As time passed, Josef Frank became increasingly critical of the way in which the modern movement developed. His criticism was primarily aimed at Germany and the Bauhaus school's overarching design ideal, which developed into a new style that required perfect conformance between building, interior, furniture, and everyday goods.

Frank rejected the idea of the architect as interpreter of the spirit of the times and the concept of the "new man." Frank's own architecture is inclusive. It does not make a clear break with tradition. It is full of contradictions, just as the modern world. In his text *Façade and Interior* from 1928, he writes: "The aim of the furnishing strived for does not consist in making the interior as rich or as simple as possible, but in making it *as comfortable as possible*: a goal that is in the middle, and so is difficult to grasp for those without any natural feeling."[5]

The central task of architecture, according to Josef Frank, is the residential building. The home should be a quiet oasis in modern society, in which one can be oneself and need not adjust to external circumstances. One of the starting points for the family house is the everyday aspect of it. At the end of his text *The House as Path and Place*, Frank places modern architecture at the heart of the trivial and the everyday, with a string of simple questions: "[. . .] the rules for the good house as an ideal do not change in principle and have only to be looked at afresh. How does one enter a garden? What does the route look like from the gateway? How does one open the front door? What is the shape of an anteroom? How does one pass the cloakroom from the anteroom to reach the living room? How does the seating area relate to the door and the window? There are many questions like these which need to be answered, and the house consists of these elements. This is modern architecture."[6]

In Josef Frank's house production, recurring themes and methods emerge. Many can already be found in his earlier projects, while others he added and developed over the years.

The first house he designed, together with Oskar Strnad and Oskar Wlach, was the Scholl House in Vienna in 1913–1914. Already in this first project there is a playful asymmetry in the fenestration of the street façade. The house has a distinct division between a tall façade towards the street and a terraced façade towards the garden. This creates a close relationship between house and garden, which Frank would repeatedly use in many subsequent projects. In the plan, the external walls follow the tapered shape of the site. A pragmatic approach that at the same time results in irregularly shaped rooms, which Frank returns to both in his writings and projects. Already in the Scholl House, there is a complex movement sequence from the street up to the entrance and then on through the house.

Garden side of the Scholl House, Vienna, 1913/14.

In the mid-1920s Frank designs a series of unrealized houses with clear modernist overtones. A common thread in these projects is that he experiments and develops different forms of movement patterns inside the houses. During the latter part of the 1920s Frank also starts experimenting with a series of houses with interior patios, where outside and inside are interwoven. This way, a kind of landscape with diagonal views and shifting levels is created. One of the most interesting houses of this type is the House for M S in Los Angeles of 1930. Unfortunately, none of these projects were realized, and it is unclear if there were real clients or if they were projects of fantasy. It is not until the 1930s that the first of Frank's more developed house projects, Villa Beer, is built in Vienna.

In the holiday town of Falsterbo on the southernmost tip of Sweden Frank designs a series of summer houses from the mid-1920s up until 1936 for his wife's family and friends. The

The roof terrace at Villa Wehtje, Falsterbo, 1936.

houses differ in size and material, but they all share the same relaxed elegance. Especially in the Claëson House and in Villa Wehjte one finds a spatial richness and variety where the movement through the houses becomes a vital part of the architectural experience. The large holiday home designed for Walter Wehtje from 1936 onwards is the last house Frank builds — and it is this house he himself was most pleased with.

In Villa Wehtje, Frank already explores ideas about chance and the accidental that he will later develop in his fantasy house designs during the 1940s and 1950s. As early as 1931, he had written: "The rectangular living room is the least suited for living in; it is very useful for furniture storage but for nothing else. I believe that if one were to draw a polygon [. . .], as a plan for a room, it would be much more functional than a regular rectangular one. In the roof ateliers the contingent factors had helped, almost always having an agreeable and impersonal effect."[7]

During the 1940s and 1950s Josef Frank designs a series of fantasy houses in which elements and expressions from earlier projects are paired with ideas of an inclusive and compound modern architecture, sometimes bordering on kitsch. Some of the fantasy house projects rank among the most interesting of Frank's designs—like the irregular Fantasy House no. 9, that Frank himself later calls "Accidental House" and which he uses as an illustration when his text *Accidentism* is published in 1958.

Amongst the themes that recur throughout the years, with varied but similar designs, is the entrance sequence into the house. The garden and sequence of outdoor spaces have a close relation with the interior. The entrance hall can consist of a single room or be divided into a sequence of rooms. There is a contrasting effect when after the small anteroom one enters a higher room, as in Villa Wehtje, or even more dramatically in Villa Beer with its high central hall.

In most of his projects, there is also a clear division between a public area with common rooms and a private area with bedrooms and facility rooms. In the anteroom or immediately afterward one is given a clear choice between these two parts.

Another theme that recurs in all of Frank's house projects is a conscious creation of movement throughout the house. The interiors are shaped by a natural sequence, and the various parts of the common rooms subtly merge without exaggerated contrasts. Frank consistently avoids long passageways or corridors in public areas. It is from these sequences, in particular, that his villas' special qualities emerge. "The route that connects these individual places in the living areas has to be diversified so that one never experiences its length. In this case various kinds of lighting conditions, steps, and other things are important aids. The opening of a door into a room is frequently of great (though often neglected) importance [. . .]."[8]

A fundamental element of Frank's design of movement through the houses is the form and placement of stairs. In some of his larger villa projects from the 1920s, there are parallel stair systems with a functionally hidden service stairway and a central, visible stair system. The central staircase in Villa Beer is an element that breaks up the dynamism and movement into various sequences in the large house. The staircase changes direction and shape and combines the different levels and spaces in the public area.

The composition of volumes can be unified as in many projects during the 1920s. Sometimes Frank uses a central master volume to which he adds smaller protrusions. This is how the Claëson house, for example, is structured. Villa Beer also has a more closed façade towards the street and a broken-up side towards the garden. In the later fantasy houses Frank tests more complex compositions of volumes.

Frank planned most of his single-family homes since the early 1920s with a roof, or parts of the roof, doubling as a terrace. In several of the summer houses the terraces are arranged as common meeting spaces. This influences the design of the floor plan, patterns of movement, and room hierarchies in a particularly dynamic way.

If the spaces in Josef Frank's projects constitute a static but dynamic design, a shell that sets the boundaries between the interior and exterior, Frank creates a kind of counterpoint interaction using furniture and interior decoration. The loose furniture defines everyday situations with varied intensity and different grades of social interaction and privacy. Frank's interiors contain a heterogeneous collection of different furniture types that cater to various needs. Often there is no correlation or clear symmetry between the individual pieces of furniture, but instead disparity and diversity in the interior "collection," creating new relationships between the furnishings and the spaces. "The living room in which one can live and think freely is neither beautiful nor harmonic nor photogenic. It is the product of coincidences; it is never finished and can accommodate everything that can fulfil the changing needs of its occupants. I use the living room as an example here because I want to employ it as a means to arrive at an architectural principle. The living room for us is, so to speak, the ultimate goal of architecture because it is the most important component of the house [...]."[9]

The exteriors of Frank's houses are often modest, in some cases almost anonymous. The interiors, meanwhile, are strikingly similar between the various projects. White-painted walls and ceiling. Often marble floors in the entrance and oak parquet flooring in other areas, either in traditional herringbone pattern or in random lengths. Brass is frequently used as an accent on handrails or in ceiling-mounted light fittings. The fireplaces are sometimes discrete in their design, but often elaborately designed with special stone cladding and brass fittings. In some cases, Frank uses solid marble slabs in horizontal niches where plants can be placed. Overall this gives Frank's interiors a light, luxurious touch. An effect that is clearly different from, for example Le Corbusier's cunning "modern" interiors.

In his popular essay *The Mathematics of the Ideal Villa*,[10] Colin Rowe shows similarities between Palladio's Villa Malcontenta and Le Corbusier's Villa in Garches in both the structural design and proportioning. Le Corbusier's plan structure with a division of the load-bearing column positions has a build-up that reminds us of Palladio's nine subdivisions of the plan. Josef Frank had studied under Karl König in Vienna and in 1910 defended his doctoral thesis on Alberti. Frank was very familiar with classical architecture and the rules and proportional principles of the renaissance. In some of Frank's projects from the 1920s there is an underlying structure that brings to mind Palladio's tripartite composition. An early example is the Claëson House, which is divided in three parts both in plan and elevation. Another example from the same time is the House for Vienna XIII, which has a plan divided in 5 by 4. In later

Hawaii, fabric design.

La Plata, fabric design.

projects as well as in the fantasy houses the underlying structure is more or less evident. It may be interesting to compare Frank's designs for printed textiles that he worked with, partly for Haus & Garten during the 1920s and for Svenskt Tenn after 1932. The textiles often have complex organic patterns of plants and flowers in winding decorative formations that were printed in up to seven colors. This requires tremendous skill in the construction of the block-printed pattern, which is repeated so that a coherent whole is achieved. Beneath the repeat patterns, which often have the character of free compositions, lies a strict structural order.[11]

Frank's architecture was also influenced by the approach developed by the Arts and Crafts Movement in England during the late nineteenth century, which directly challenged symmetrical and classical solutions in favor of an additive and irregular architecture. Hermann Muthesius's book *The English House* [*Das englische Haus*] was highly influential on the continent. The book *Houses and Gardens* by the English architect Mackay Hugh Baillie Scott was published in German in 1912 and deeply impressed Frank and his contemporaries Oskar Strnad and Oskar Wlach. The interior design company Frank started in 1925 with Oskar Wlach was given the analogous name "Haus & Garten." One element from the English house that Baillie Scott stresses in particular and that lives on and develops in new interpretations of Frank's architecture is "The Living Hall"—a central hall that is the house's heart and focal point, often extending over two floors with a fireplace and lounge suite furniture. Variations of this type of room can be found both in Villa Beer and Villa Wehtje, in many of his earlier houses and later in the fantasy houses. Frank also examines these ideas in smaller houses such as his detached house at the Werkbundsiedlung housing exhibition 1932 in Vienna, which has a living room that continues via the staircase to the floor above and out onto a roof terrace.

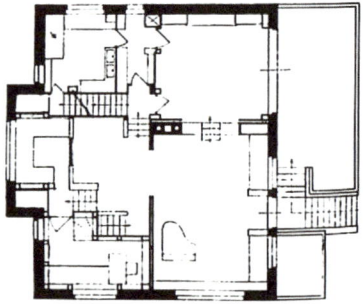

Plan drawing Haus Moller, Vienna, 1927/28. Architect Adolf Loos.

In his architecture Josef Frank was concerned with aspects of space. Many of his buildings are a combination of modern dynamic space and a plan organization that is reminiscent of Camillo Sitte's diagrams of medieval squares and urban spaces as well as Alberti's theories. In the text *The House as Path and Place*, Frank states that we should move through a house as if it was a small city: narrow alleys ending on open spaces, which in turn lead to new passages.

Frank also took inspiration from Adolf Loos's architecture and his *Raumplan*[12] principle. Although Loos's architecture is different from Frank's in many respects, there are similarities in the winding staircases found in their houses, the dramatic interplay of high open spaces and more intimate lower areas. Loos develops his interiors so that every room has its own logic with symmetry and different materials used on wall panels and fixed furniture. He gives static rooms a dynamic relationship to each other, so that a three-dimensional spatial puzzle is formed.

Frank's interiors have a more dynamic and less formal character. They seldom have the same compact, economical density that many of Loos's houses exhibit. There is also a spatial-psychological aspect, originated by Loos and developed by Frank, which differs from the mechanical objectivity and rational ideals of the 1920s. A route through the house does not have to be as short as possible, and the size of a room is not the only criterion for its usability. Movement through a space is seen as a quality-generating aspect in its own right.

In his text *Accidentism,* Josef Frank writes that "we should design our surroundings as if they originated by chance."[13] What Frank proposes is not arbitrariness or random architecture, but an intellectual method that allows the architect to be inclusive, pragmatic, complex, humorous, and elegant, all at the same time.

Josef Frank has been a "minor classic" and an architect for architects. Today we see a new interest in Frank's work among a young generation of architects. Perhaps the time is ripe for Josef Frank to have a broader impact and receive recognition as one of the twentieth century's most significant architects and thinkers.

1 Roland Barthes. *La chambre claire. Note sur la photographie,* 1980 (*Camera Lucida. Reflections on Photography,* 1981).
2 See Claudia Cavallar. "Josef Frank Chairs" in *Josef Frank: Against Design,* 2016, pp. 185–197.
3 See Nina Stritzler-Levine. "Three Visions of the Modern Home: Josef Frank, Le Corbusier and Alvar Aalto" in *Josef Frank. Architect and Designer,* 1996, pp. 16–29: 22–24.
4 Frank. "Frippery for the Soul and Frippery as a Problem" (1927) in *Josef Frank. Writings, vol. 1,* 2012, pp. 289–299: 299.
5 Frank. "Façade and Interior" (1928) in *Josef Frank. Writings, vol. 1,* pp. 347–351: 347.
6 Frank. "The House as Path and Place" (1931) in *Josef Frank. Writings, vol. 2,* 2012, pp. 199–209: 209.
7 Ibid.: 201.
8 Ibid.: 207.
9 Frank. "Accidentism" (1958) in *Josef Frank. Writings, vol. 2,* pp. 373–387: 377.
10 The essay was first published in *The Architectural Review* in 1947. It was later included in the book with the same name (1976).
11 See Claudia Cavallar and Sebastian Hackenschmidt. "The Freer the Pattern, the Better. Josef Frank's Fabric Designs" in *Josef Frank: Against Design,* pp. 249–259: 249.
12 On Adolf Loos's *Raumplan* see Dietrich Worbs (ed.). Der *Raumplan* von Adolf Loos, 1983; or Max Risselada (ed.). *Raumplan versus Plan Libre,* 1988.
13 Frank. "Accidentism," op. cit.: 385.

Case Study 1

Claëso
House
Falster
1924-1

Perspective drawing by Frank.

n
bo
927

Villa Claëson, picture from early years.

Case Study 1
Claëson House, Falsterbo, 1924–1927

Summer house for Signhild and Axel Claëson,
Rostockervägen 1, Falsterbo

The Claëson House is an example of the interest in 1920s' Europe for modern architecture to address elements of ship design. With its railings and cabin it resembles a ship stranded on the Falsterbo sand dunes. The sea is close by, and when the house was built, the water was visible from all directions except the north in an otherwise completely open landscape. The site's special qualities have been incorporated into the project and developed into a dynamic spatial context both on the ground floor with its public areas and outdoor terraces, and the roof terrace's social areas as well as its access via a circular staircase.

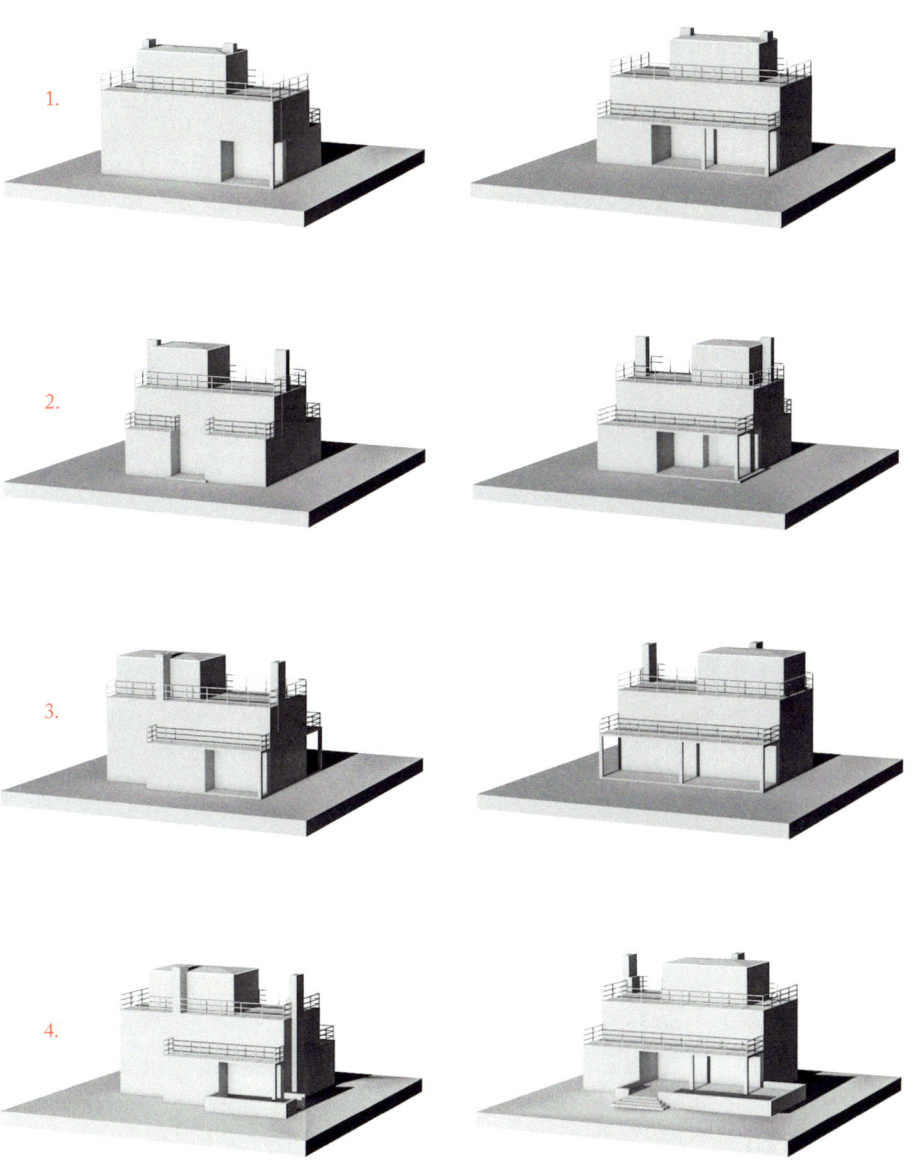

Views of the four versions, from west and east.

The house was presented in issue 31 of the journal *Deutsche Kunst und Dekoration* in 1928 together with the text *Fassade und Interieur* [Façade and interior].

Process
Functionalism made a broader impact in Sweden only with the Stockholm Exhibition of 1930. The Claëson House is one of Sweden's very early examples of a single-family house that, in its volume build-up and detailing, establishes a link to early modernism in Europe.

The house was built in 1927 for Frank's sister-in-law, Signhild, and her husband Axel Claëson. Frank made several proposals for the house during the project's relatively long design phase, which started in 1924. It is only in the fourth sketch proposal that Frank's plan solution achieves the desired functional and geometric clarity that the house now exhibits in its built state.

The differences between the various versions lie mainly in the internal stair positioning and design, and in how this affects the ground and the upper bedroom floor. It is highly interesting to observe in the design process how the penthouse developed from an attic storage space to a roof terrace with areas for socializing connected to a studio. This was made possible by moving the main staircase to the center of the house in the built version and having it lead all the way up to the terrace.

When Josef Frank was interviewed a few years later in 1929 for the Swedish weekly *Vecko-Journalen* on the Claëson House, he described, among other things, the structure's relationship to the site: It "[...] was important to give the building, which is located on the heathland towards the sea, protection from the sea and its storms, but also the best views over it. Thus, large continuous windows towards the sea and for calmer days a balcony and a terrace on this side. In fact, the house 'lives' on the other side, towards the greenery. It is

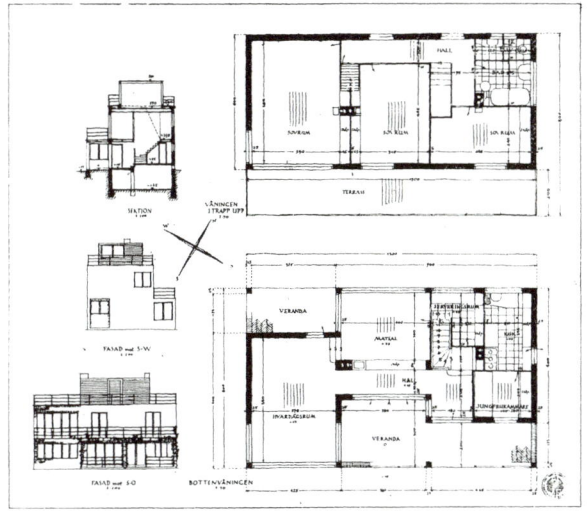

Plans and façades, first version, original drawing.

Plans and façades, second version, original drawing.

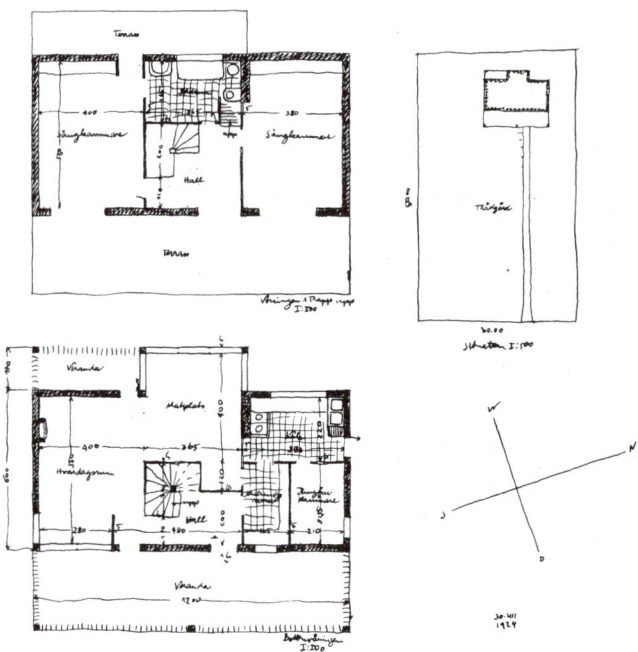

Plans and façades, third version, original drawing.

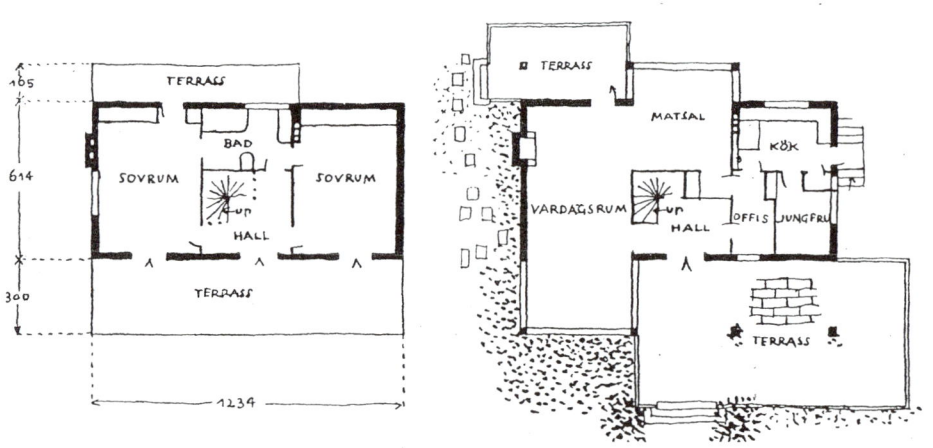

Plans, built version.

here that the garden is located as well as a large ground-floor terrace with comfortable seating. It is also in this direction that the bedrooms on the upper floor open towards the large balcony to take in the sun and air. [...] The small cabin or studio at the top is painted-gray timber, which might have, if it had been built with handmade bricks, become too heavy for the building."

Plan principle
Several of Frank's houses are planned on the basis of a principle similar to the one we see in the Claëson House. In continuation of the interview above, Frank describes his design process: "The house's frame, in other words, that which is bounded by the foundation walls, is smaller than one imagines when one [first] sees the house. [...] In order to create more space I often use built-out 'pockets.' So, for example, the dining room is composed mostly of a 'pocket,' and on the other side in the living room is also a large built-out bookcorner, wall to wall with the terrace."

View of the interior, living room.

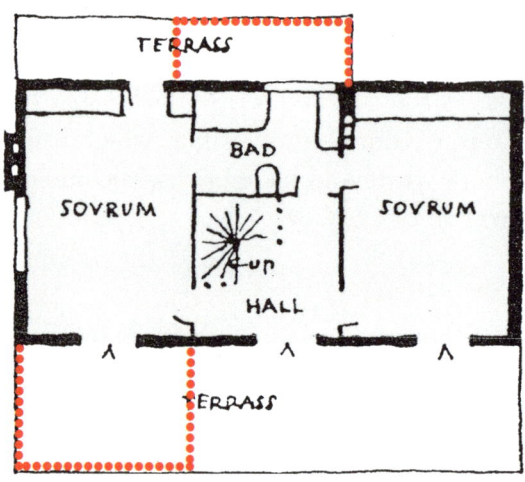
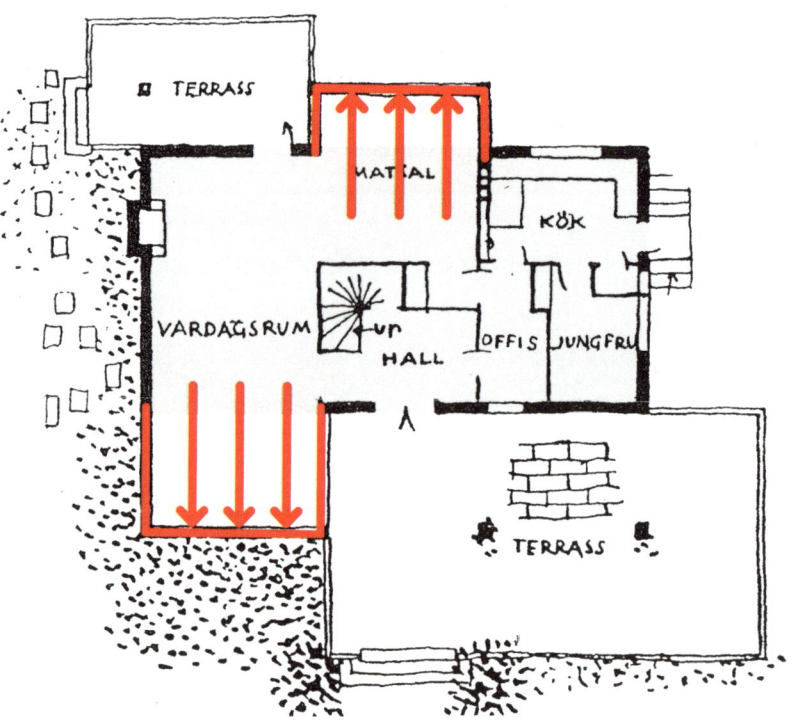

Plan principle referring to Frank's quote about his working method.

Perhaps especially interesting is to spare a thought for Frank's working method, because it is documented in *Vecko-Journalen*'s interview. The different sketches clearly show how the house, step by step, is reworked in accordance with his method.

He starts with a mostly right-angled main volume and manipulates it by pulling out boxes, i.e. rooms, from it. He creates a varied and complex building, both functionally and in terms of design, based on a simple rectangular building form. The basic volume remains clearly readable, holding together the whole project.

In the Claëson House, the centrally placed spiral staircase is the hub that loosely binds together the public areas on the ground floor and connects the terraces at ground level with the roof terrace and the studio, which are both vital during the summer season. The living room is like a box that has been drawn out from the main volume and becomes a glazed part of the terrace next to the entrance. A similar extraction is made for the dining room on the western side of the house. In the completed proposal, the terraces at ground level are enlarged, creating an extension of the house's plan. The terraces are partially covered by a roof, defined and demarcated from the rest of the garden through low brick walls.

Room sequences and the approach to the house
Josef Frank's villas often have a close connection to the gardens. In the Claëson House, the sequence of outdoor rooms has a relation to its internal organization. The structure is slightly elevated in relation to the walkway that leads up to the entrance. A few steps leading up to the terrace clearly demarcate the garden with a low brick wall and the living room's projecting glazed section. A large part of the veranda is covered by the upper terrace, which is supported by the living room and two sturdy brick pillars. In this way, the terrace or balcony on the upper floor becomes a kind of large portico-like entrance canopy. In the sequence of movement

Garden and entrance façade seen from the east.

View of the interior, entrance hall.

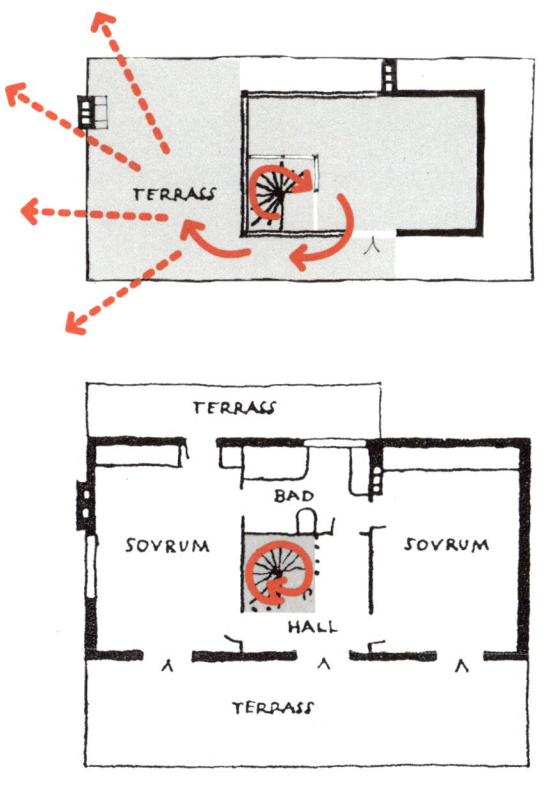
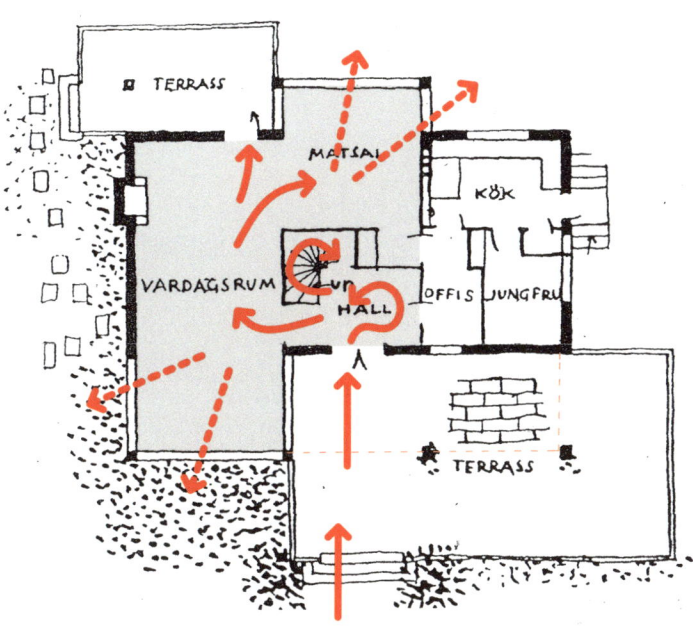

Approach to the house. Room sequences inside, ground floor to the terrace level. Views.

into the house this becomes a transition zone that conveys the meeting between inside and outside.

Nevertheless, this transition is both clearly defined and fluent. Defined through the restricted door openings, fluent because the outdoor room intertwines with the stairwell under the terrace's roof, causing the veranda to be fully integrated into the building's overall structure.

Inside the glazed double doors we immediately arrive at the heart or center of the house—the small stairwell—and are presented with two possibilities: either go through a relatively narrow passage leading to the living room or take the stairs up to the private areas and further up to the roof terrace with its studio. In the hall, the two possibilities are emphasized just as much as the room's spatial form, whose unusual design produces an ambivalent impression. Both the living room and the stairs invite us further in by way of the incidence of daylight. The living room has a dynamic effect, with distinctly lighter and darker parts, which guides us further around the staircase towards the bright dining area to the west. The staircase is lit beautifully from above. In the hall, it is difficult to get an idea of the rooms' relationships and of what the end goal may be. We are encouraged to continue forward.

Light—dark
In the Claëson House, we find a clear example of how Frank consciously distributes the light and dark areas of the rooms, and how this contributes to the dynamics of the floor plan and a varied spatial experience for the public areas. Between the well-lit reading area and the clear dining area lies the dark corner of the fireplace. In addition, subtle differences, for example in windowsill heights, division of windows, etc., contribute to a multifaceted spatial experience. In the dining room, the large undivided window with views out to the sea has a lower windowsill. There are slightly higher sills with divided windows in the reading area, where there would be

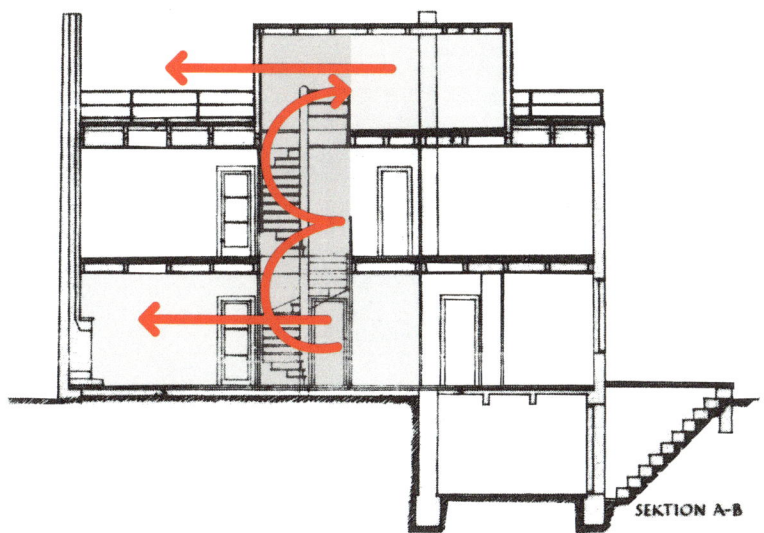

Section. Room sequence from the living area on the ground floor up to the common space on the rooftop terrace. Views.

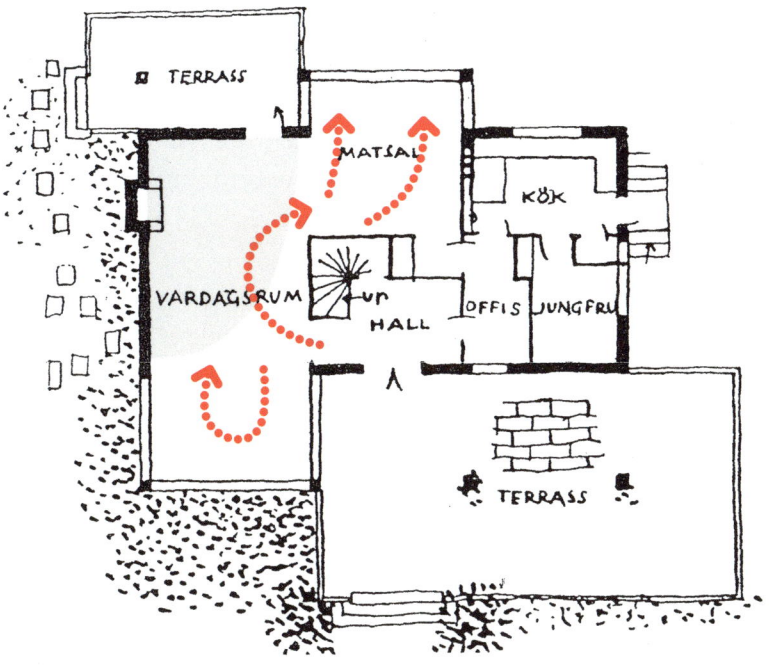

Daylight of the interior. Brighter parts in the bay windows and darker part of the living area around the fireplace.

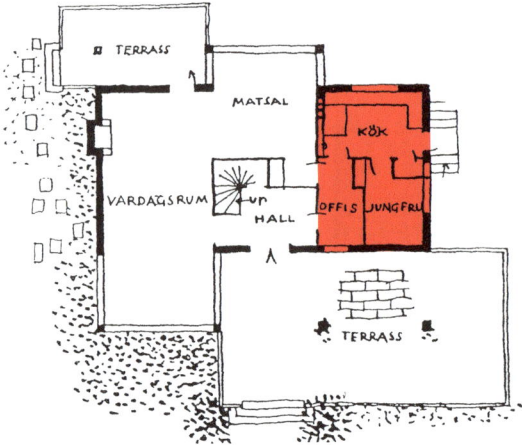

Service space on entrance floor in relation to the living area.

furniture under the windows. That causes this part of the room to feel turned inwards on itself despite the large openings.

In Frank's larger house projects from this period we find intricate patterns of movement and complex room contexts. Even in such a small project as the Claëson House, there is a clear path through the house and the impression of a not immediately foreseeable gathering space, bringing deliberate complexity and dynamism to the project.

Arrangement of plans
The plan of the Claëson House is a good example of the theme Frank developed for smaller houses. The floor plan relates to one of his other summer houses, Carlsten House, in Falsterbo, and this theme can be found even in sketches for several of his projects from 1910 onward and from the 1920s. He designed a plan that in the best possible way satisfied the accommodation's different forms, functions, and movement. The drawn-out building elements help to differentiate and enlarge the interior of the house. The upper level shows what Frank calls

Picture from south-east, early years.

the "basic shape," i.e. a rectangular volume without the extractions and recesses that characterize the ground floor.

Proportions and façades
As for the design of the building's exterior, Frank describes his approach in the interview mentioned above: "I completely conceptualize the house as a whole before I build it with a conscious balance of the rooms following the façades' proportions. I do not strive for obvious symmetry, therefore one of the house's gables has no windows on the upper floor and the other one none on the ground floor."

Frank believes that proportions are the only way to create harmony. He describes the volume of the Claëson House as an area bounded by the "foundation wall." By this he means the rectangular plan over two floors without the protruding glazed bays and terraces. The rectangle corresponds in plan to two squares whose sides are c. 6.14 m, thus 6.14 × 12.34 m. This volume can be divided into three equal parts, of which two thirds contain the living and dining areas, the third part the kitchen and service area. The bedroom floor also follows

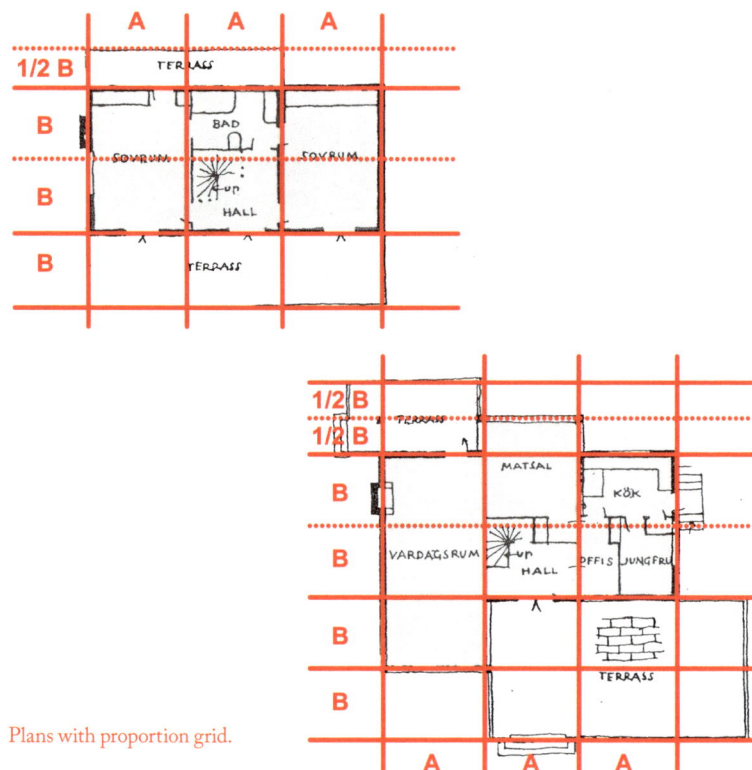

Plans with proportion grid.

this relation. The plan's tripartite division is integrated into the house's outer volume build-up and façade design—that which Frank calls the house's "prime volume." The gables of the house are as tall as they are wide, i.e. the height to width ratio is 1:1. The main volume's long façades can be divided into two squares, i.e. 1:2. The heart of the structure—the main volume—and the protruding verandas and terraces have a proportional relationship to one another. The terraces and balconies are closely connected to the house and are part of Frank's overall proportioning system, not something that is added to the house.

Frank describes the house as not generally having symmetry both in the façades and in the subdivisions. The gables have different window arrangements; the west-facing façade

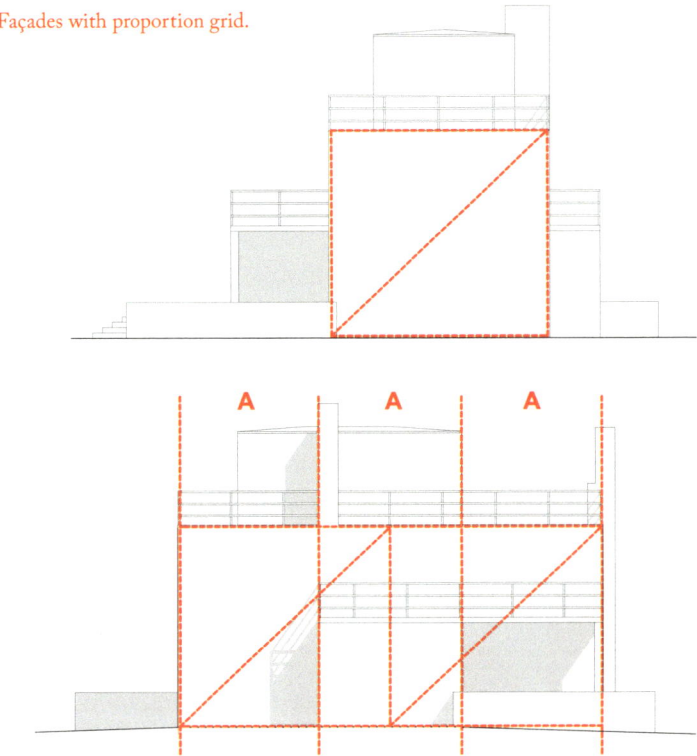

Façades with proportion grid.

shows a free distribution of walls and windows. If we look closer at the east-facing façade, we see the seemingly symmetrical window-door motif pushed out of its apparent order.

It is interesting to reflect on this deliberate aim at symmetrical disorder together with the clear order and clarity found in the house's proportioning system, in regards to both the volume-creating elements and the windows and doors.

Frank's projects both from the 1910s and from the 1920s often possess well-proportioned plans—e.g. two squares. Claëson House and Villa Bunzl in Ortmann, for example, have the same base dimensions: 6×12 m. Frank believed that a good dimensional relationship should be as simple as possible (e.g. height, width, length in a ratio of 1:2:4).

Case Study 2

House Vienna XIII 1926

Perspective drawing, 1926.

for

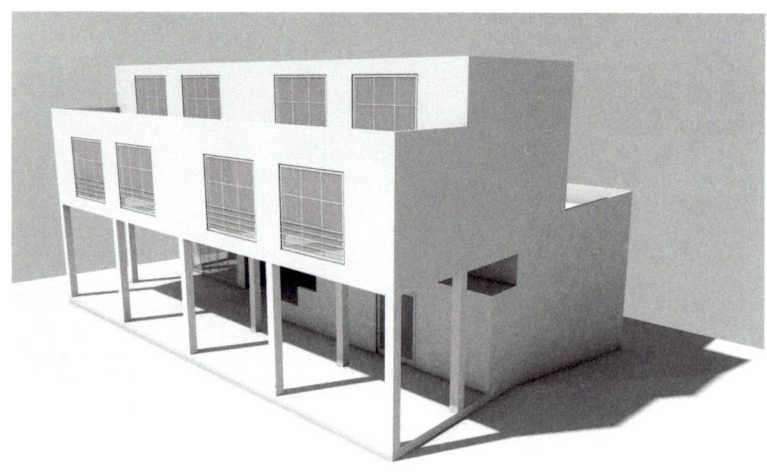

Rendering.

Case Study 2
House for Vienna XIII, 1926

Unbuilt project

This project is one of Frank's most complex designs from the mid-1920s. A covered outdoor terrace on the ground floor is linked with an open roof terrace via a patio-like courtyard that extends vertically through the entire house. An intricate system of internal and external stairs guides through the structure.

Building volume
The house is composed of three main volumes: a rectangular one contains basement and ground floor; raised on columns, there is a second rectangular volume with a central recessed courtyard; at the top, a third volume overlaps the second one and the courtyard. Together they form an external, diagonal route through the house.

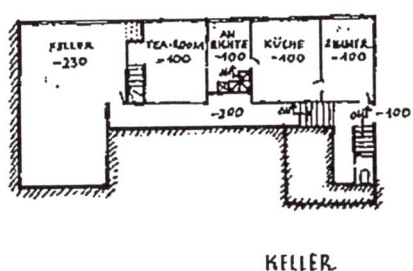
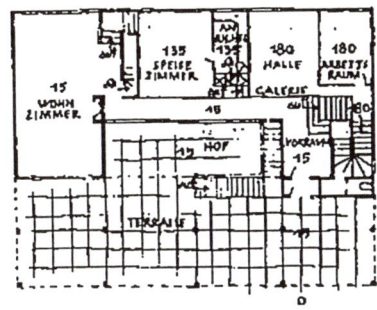
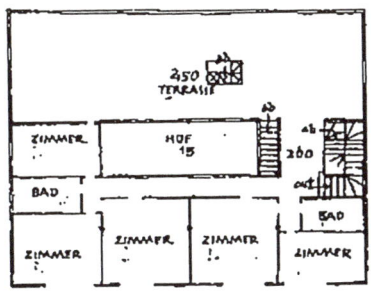
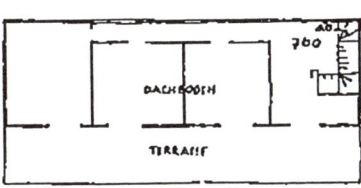
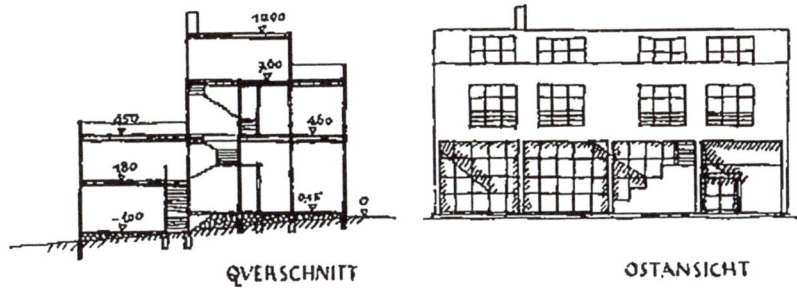

Original plans, section and elevation, 1926.

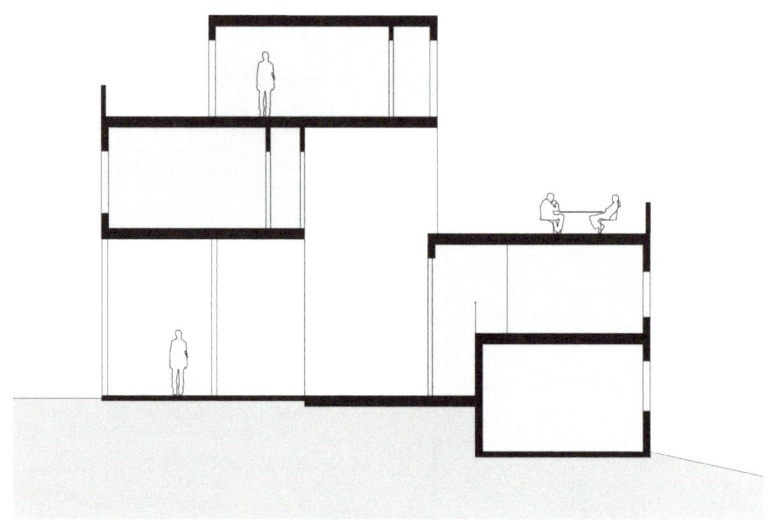

Section showing the three overlapping volumes.

Rendering towards the diagonal courtyard.

Levels
The whole building composition is spread out over eight different levels. The public areas are distributed in an intricate network across the floors. The entrance and living room are located on the same level. From the entrance, a glazed walkway extends along the external terrace. To reach the tearoom in the basement, a staircase leads down from the living room, turning by 90 degrees to the left and then 90 degrees to the right. From the rear part of the living room, another staircase leads up to the dining room.

The dining room is connected to a pantry, a dumb waiter, and a narrow spiral staircase that leads down to the kitchen in the basement. The same service stairs and dumb waiter continue up to the roof terrace above. Another narrow staircase leads past the dining room to the gallery and study. Here, and from the walkway between the entrance and living room, one can access a staircase that first turns by 180 degrees and then 90 degrees, finally opening onto the roof terrace. While the roof terrace is visually connected to the entrance terrace via the open courtyard, an external staircase also provides a direct functional connection.

The house, with its complex web of rooms, does not achieve the same relaxed and natural flow as the patio house projects, for example House for M S in Los Angeles or Villa Wehtje. Frank seems to stand with one foot in something older and more static and with the other one in early modernism's more liberated spatial relationships without really being able to decide on a direction.

Program – division
In this design, service functions, private and public areas are intertwined in a way that is rather unusual for Frank's houses. On the first floor and on the upper floor the division is clearer, while in the lower parts of the house the program is more entwined.

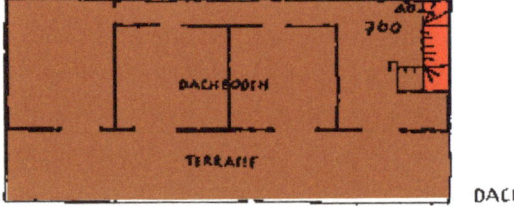

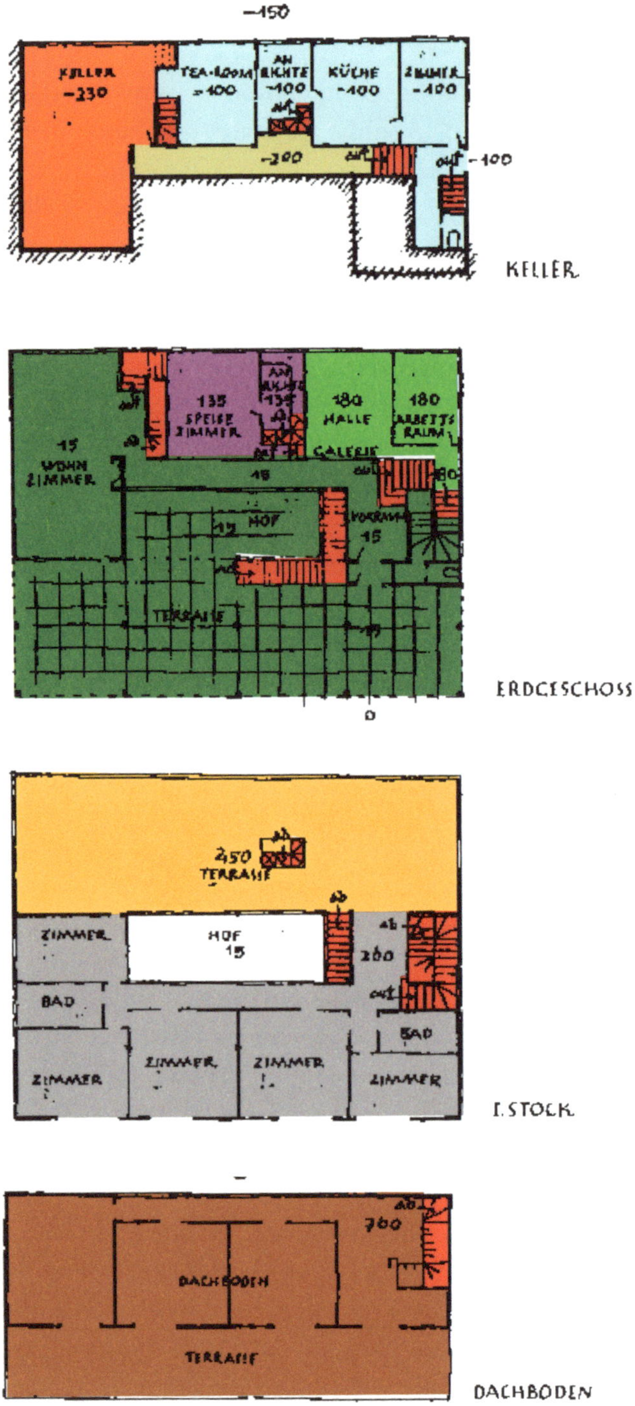

Plans with the eight different levels in different colors.

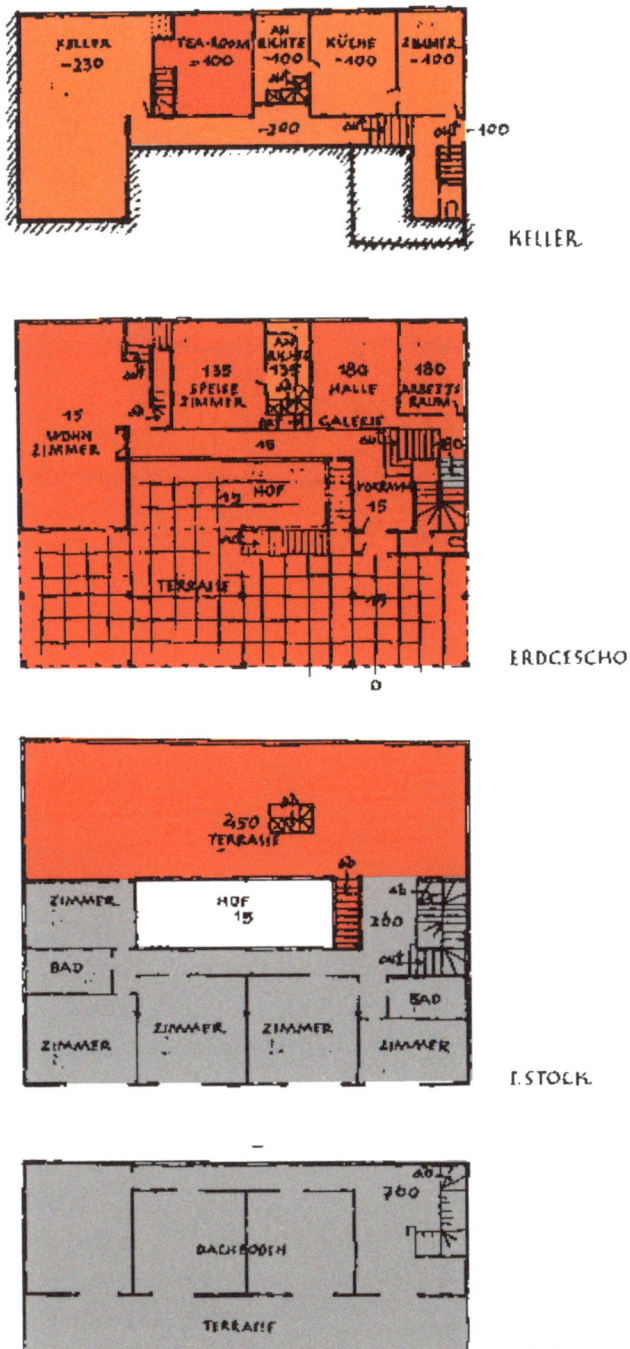

Plans with service area in orange, public areas in red, and private areas in gray.

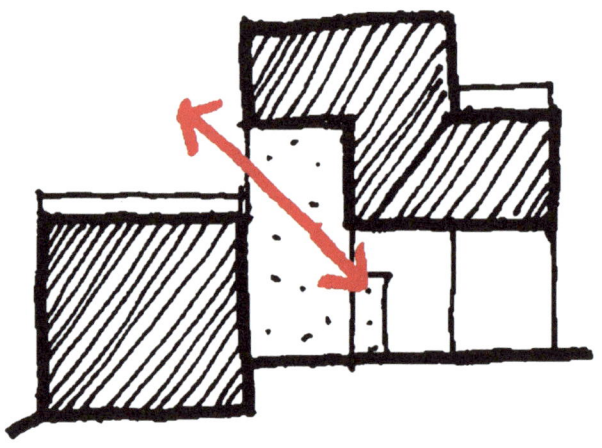

The diagonal courtyard with view from entrance level to roof terrace.

The diagonal courtyard
The idea of a diagonal courtyard that runs through the building volume is taken up again by Frank in some of his fantasy houses from the 1940s. In Fantasy House no. 10 a lower area is combined with an interior patio and with another volume raised up on pillars. Here the diagonal movement through the house takes place on the inside, around the staircase that is situated in the overlapping parts of the house. Fantasy House no. 13 also shows similarities with the House for Vienna XIII by way of an elevated portion, a portion on the ground, and an overlap between them. Here the raised portion is an octagonal courtyard-like recess.

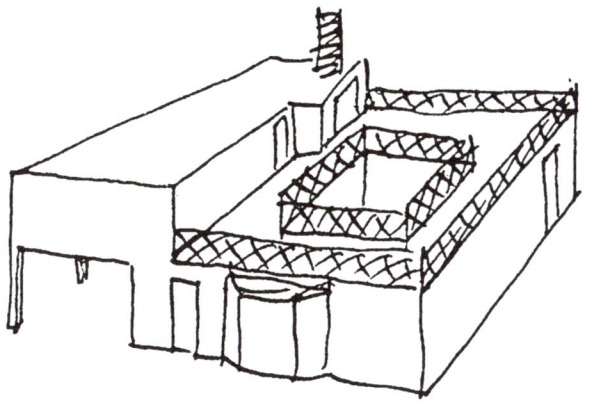

Sketch of Fantasy House no. 10 with courtyard and raised volume, 1947.

Watercolor of Fantasy House no. 13 with courtyard and raised volume, 1947.

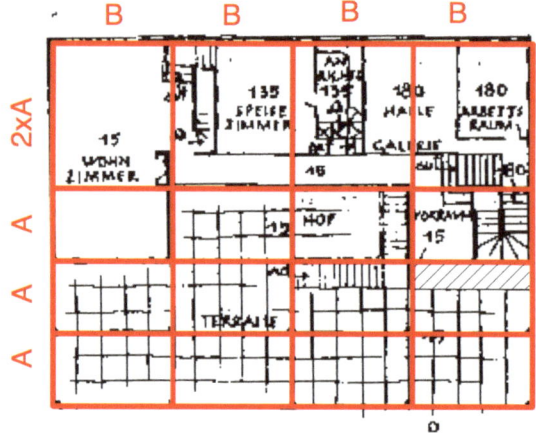

Drawings with proportion grid.

Stairs

This project is one of the most complex among Frank's designs in terms of staircase solutions. A system of different stairs enables communication between and within the public, private, and service areas in manifold ways:

Stair *B* and the dumb waiter lead from the kitchen basement up through the house to the roof terrace on the first floor;

Stair *C* leads from the basement up to the ground floor;

Stairs *D* and *A* both lead from the living room down to the tearoom in the basement and to the dining room;

Stair *E* is a narrow staircase between the dining room and the gallery; the external *Stair G* and internal *Stair F* both lead from the entrance terrace to the roof terrace;

and *Stair H* runs in between the bedrooms on the first floor to the rooms on the top floor.

Proportions, plans, and façades

The rectangular plan form is divided into four parts (4B) in width and five parts in height (5A). There are few deviations from the strict geometry in plan and in the volume's structure. Even the height of the façades and sections follows the same division.

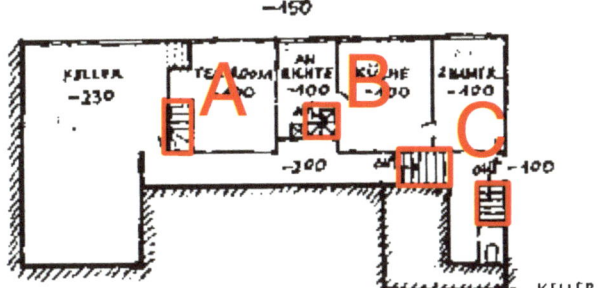
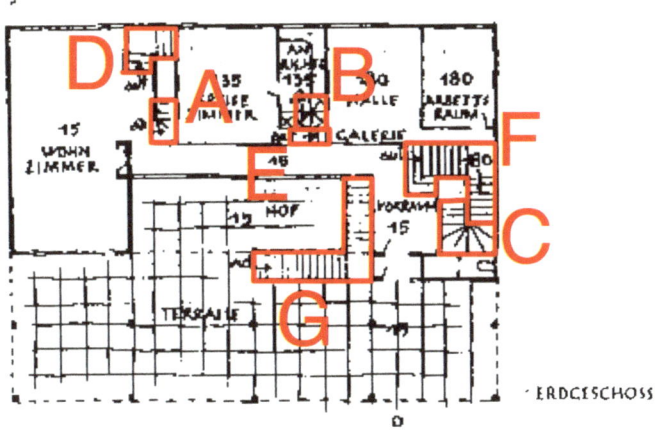
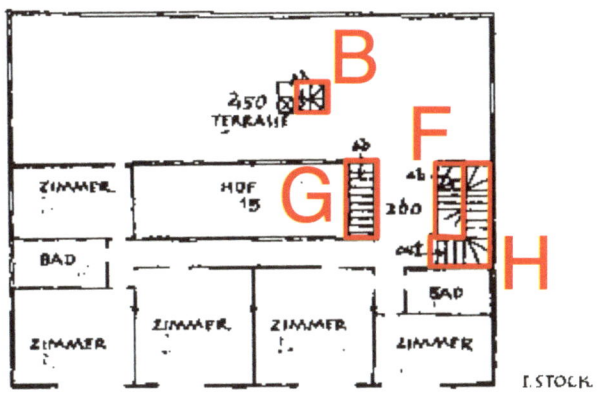

Stairs A to H.

Case Study 3

House for MS Los An 1930

Original plan.

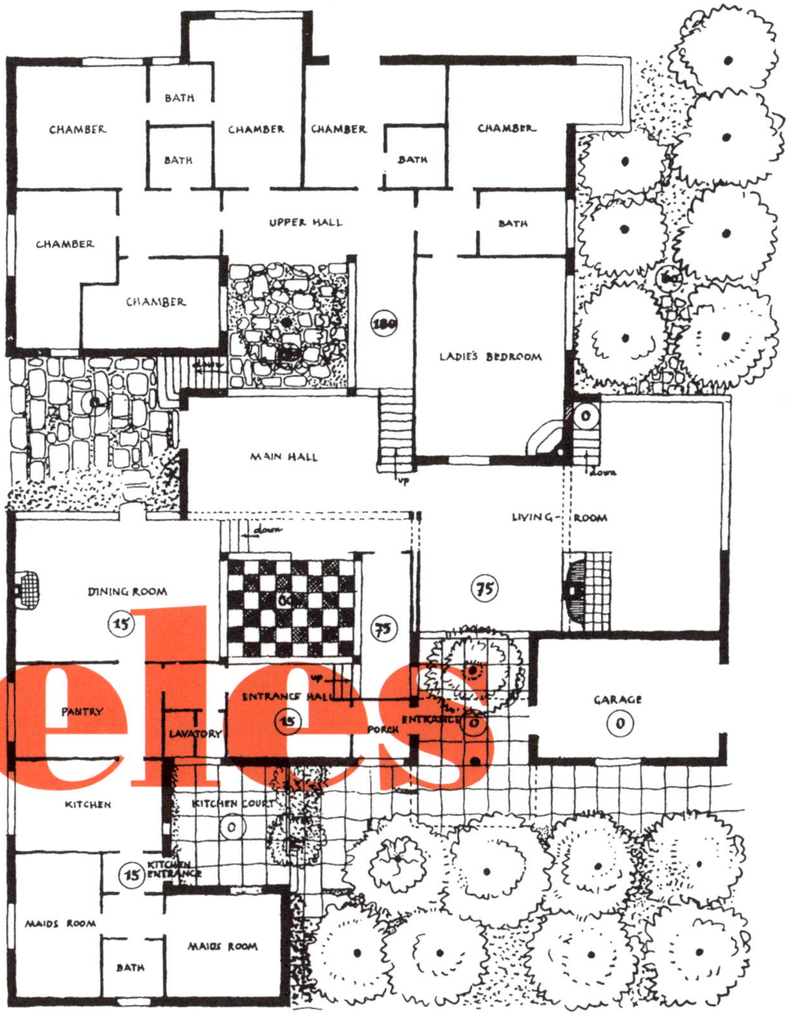

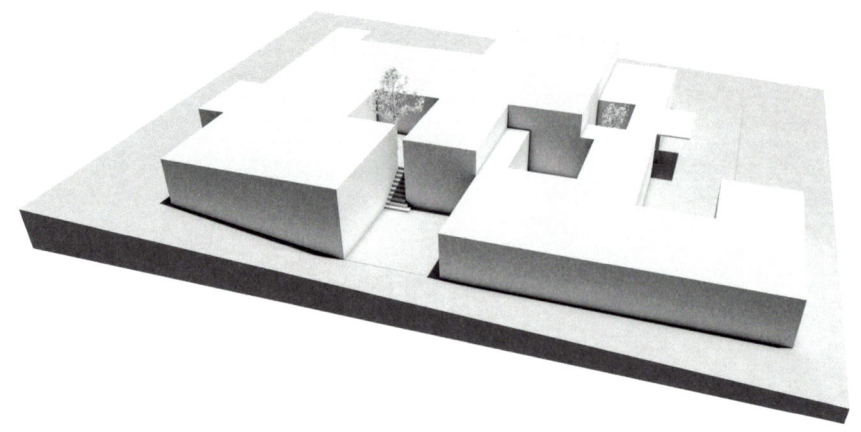

Second version, 1930. Renderings of volumes.

Case Study 3
House for M S, Los Angeles, 1930

Unbuilt project

It is unclear who the client M S was. In 1930 Frank designed three different versions for a large bungalow in Los Angeles. The first variation is reminiscent of Villa Wehtje in its approach with an irregular courtyard located between three volumes. The two later versions are patio houses, which in varying ways are designed around interior patios and in a radical way bring the outdoors to the center of the building.

Around the same time, Frank experimented with diverse solutions for interior patios in a number of other projects. Unfortunately, none of these projects were realized.

Building volume (second version)
The house is situated on a sloping site and consists of two clearly distinct parts. Part A with the main entrance lies at the

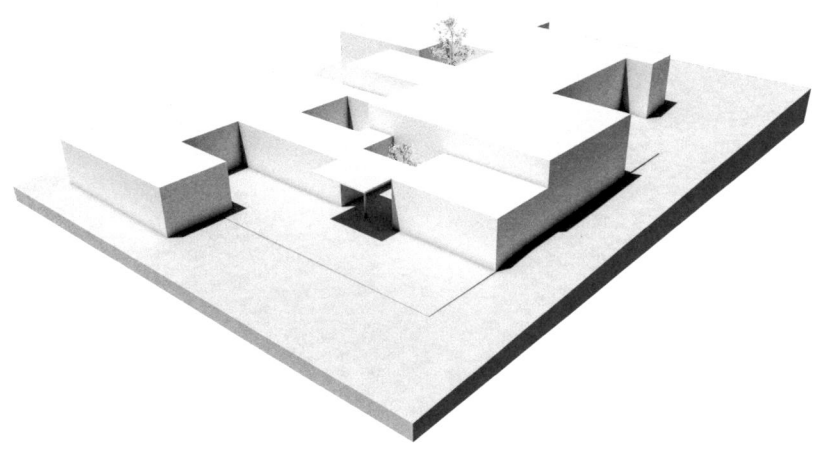

site's lowest level, while part B lies higher up; the connecting center portion is characterized by a double ceiling height.

Volume A contains the porch, entrance hall, and the service areas with kitchen courtyard, staff areas, and a garage. These rooms have a ceiling height of 2.5 m. A fully glazed patio is framed by the dining room and a hallway, which leads into the double-height center section containing the living room and the main hall in irregular shape. A large open fireplace divides the living room into two parts.

Movement
The visitor moves towards the entrance via a large courtyard on the lowest level of the site and enters the building under a ceiling panel supported by a central pillar. This umbrella-like panel is detached from the surrounding walls, allowing natural light to fall onto a large tree. As soon as one enters the door, the first patio becomes visible. In the entrance hall one makes a U-turn and proceeds up four steps to the level of the checker-patterned patio. The movement continues through the house around the patio and out into the double-height space of the central hallway and living room.

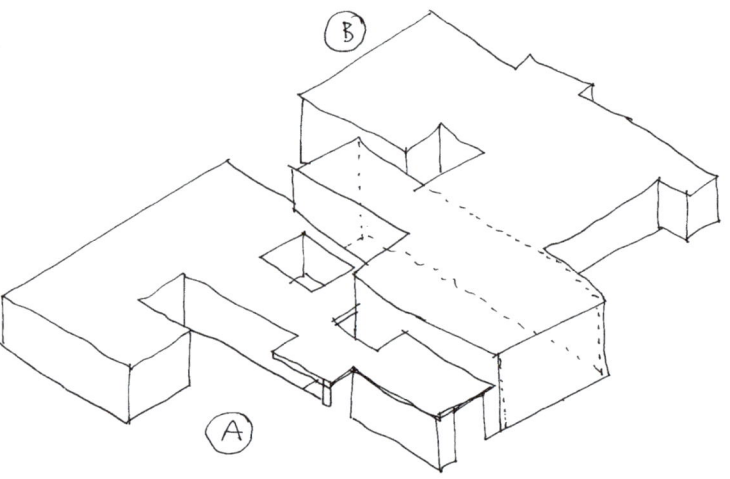

A. Entrance and service volume. B. Volume with public areas and private bedrooms.

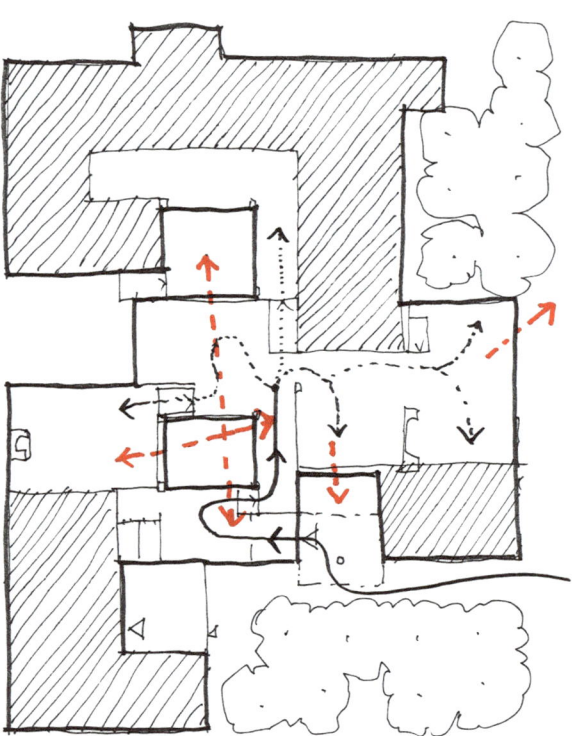

Path into the house to public and private areas in black. Views through rooms and courtyards in red.

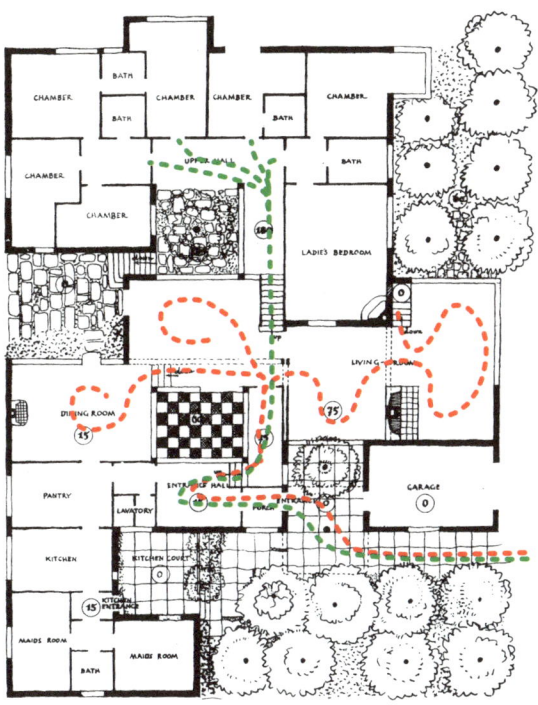

Path through the house to public areas in red and to private rooms in green.

A staircase leads from the hall up to the private spaces of the house with bedrooms, wardrobes, and bathrooms. The rooms in this part are grouped around a second patio. It is situated at the same level as the bedrooms but is visible from the entrance hall through windows placed at a high level.

Frank works in a masterly way, varying the closed and open areas of the house. Movement up through the house takes a natural form with both patios becoming distinct and central elements in the house's architectural layout.

Program—functions
As in most of Frank's other single-family houses, the private and the public areas, as well as the service functions are clearly

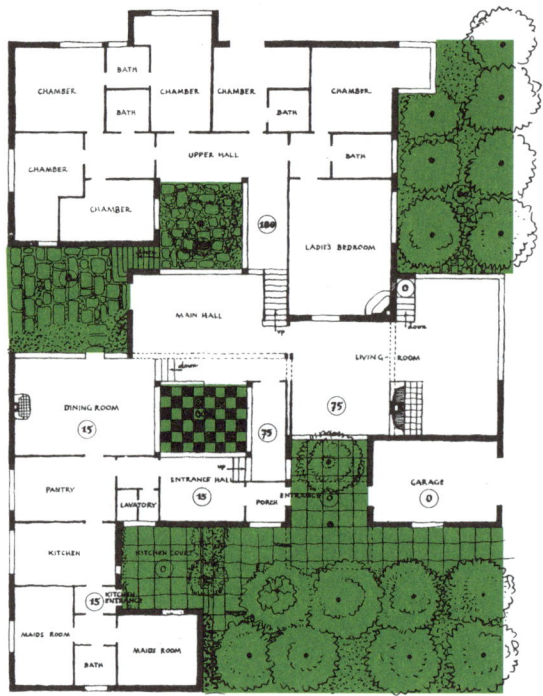

Plan with exterior areas in green.

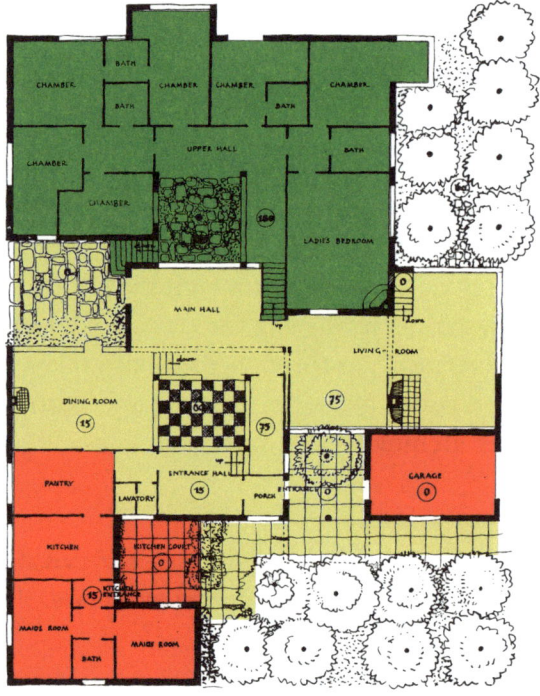

Service areas in red, public spaces in yellow, private rooms in green.

separated. In the House for M S all the rooms are located next to each other (instead of on top of each other as is the case e.g. in Villa Beer), and there is a certain visual interweaving of the various functions.

Level differences
There is a general difference of 1.8 m between the highest and the lowest floor. In between Frank arranges the groups of functions on three different levels according to the gradient of the site. So the house literally creeps up the sloping site, and the interior becomes a constructed landscape with partly intimate areas, partly grand views to the outside and spaces with high ceilings. This constitutes a different approach to giving shape to the ideas in the text *The House as Path and Place* than in Villa Beer, where the spatial configuration to a large degree occurs vertically.

Inside—outside
The relationship between outside and inside is interwoven in a refined manner. Through the two patios the outside becomes a part of the whole architecture. The folded façade with its different U-shaped courtyards also creates alcoves and corners that reinforce the relationship between inside and outside. Through careful placement of the window openings, views are either amplified or screened.

Different versions
Version 1 of this house plan differs from the two later ones. In this version, the house is divided into two distinct volumes which are grouped around an elongated serpentine courtyard. It is unclear wether this version was intended for the same site as the latter two. The lower area with a lounge has a fully glazed wall facing the garden. The dining room table is placed in an alcove with a curved screen that can lead us to think of Mies van der Rohe's curved dining room wall in

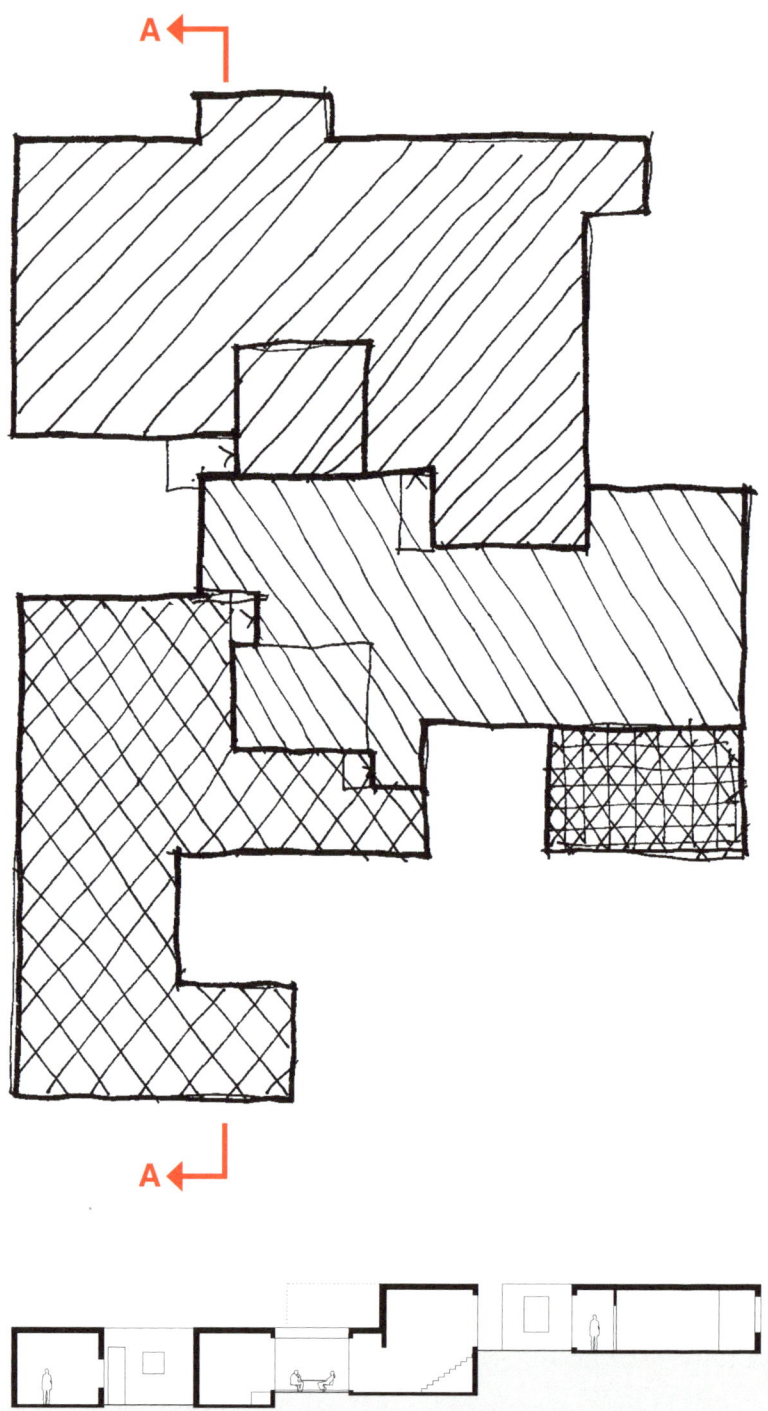

Plan with different levels. Section through house and courtyards.

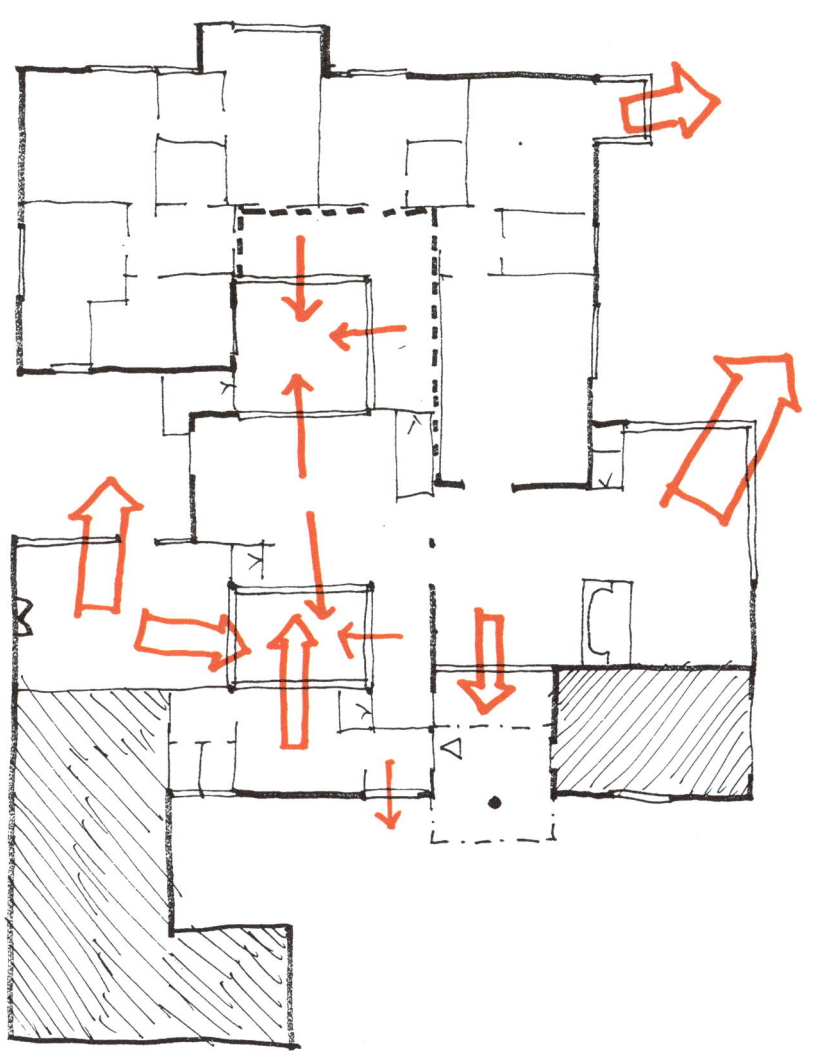

Different focuses and views from the interior to the exterior in different parts of the house.

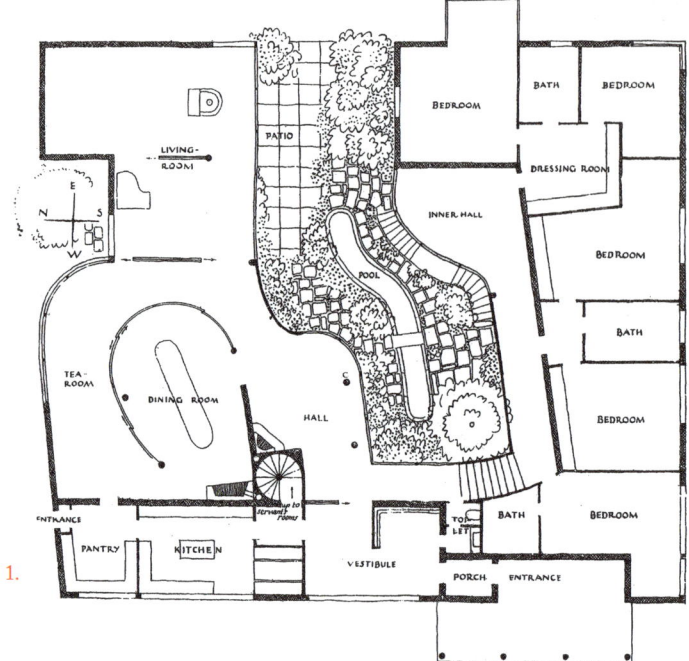

1.

Three different versions.

Villa Tugendhat from the same year. At a higher level is the private area of the house with bedrooms, dressing room, and bathrooms. The overall footprint is an anticipation of Villa Wehtje, which Frank first designed in 1936.

The second version of the project is substantially different from the previous one. The house plan has right angles, and instead of a large courtyard, Frank uses two patios and several recesses as spaces between the building's different parts. In this project the house climbs up the sloping site over three levels.

The third version of the project resembles the second but groups the lounge with a larger part of the overall surface. The dining and living rooms are more clearly separated, and the project contains many small niches and intimate spaces either to get together or seek privacy.

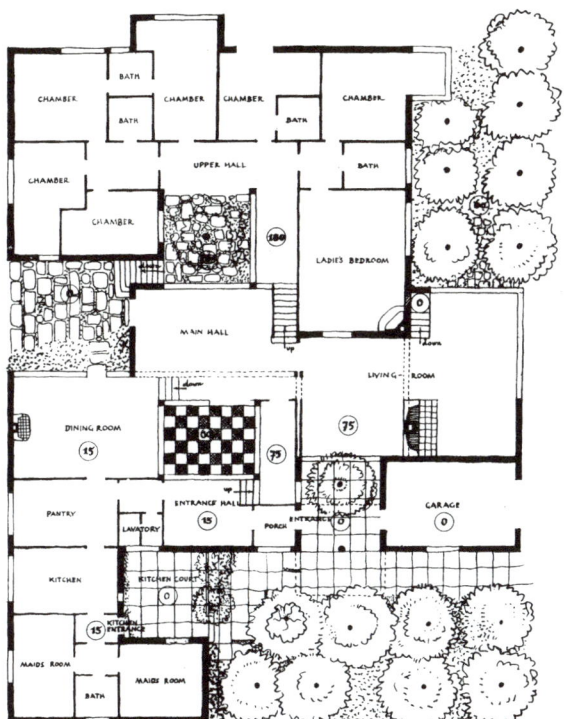

2.

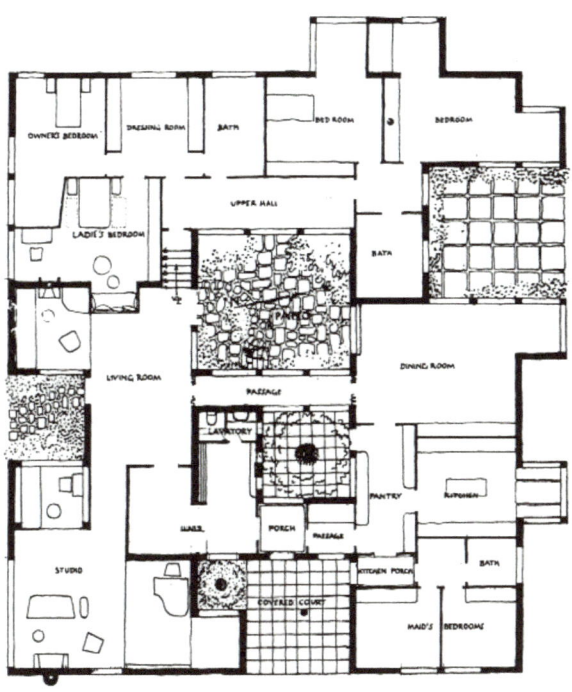

3.

Case Study 4

Villa Beer Vienna 1930

Entrance side towards Wenzgasse.

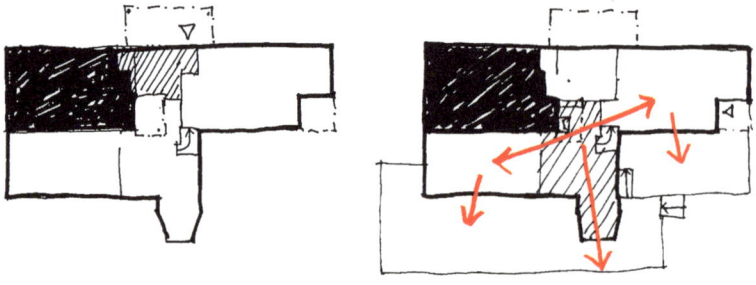

Left: Plan with service area in black, entrance area in gray, and main public spaces in white. Right: Plan showing main views from dining room through main hall towards living room and vice versa. All three spaces also provide views to the garden.

Case Study 4
Villa Beer, Vienna, 1930

Villa for Julius and Margarete Beer, Wenzgasse 12, Vienna XIII. In collaboration with Oskar Wlach

This large house over five floors has a rather closed façade towards the street and opens up with large glazed elements and broken-up volumes towards the garden. The tall central hall is the hub of the house around which the public areas are grouped on different levels. The central staircase winds its way up through the house in different directions and turns.

Organization–program
As in most of Frank's villas the different functions are clearly separated: service areas with kitchen and servants' living quarters in one part; circulation areas and staircase in another part; public spaces such as dining room, hall, living room, music room, and library at the center of the house. The private spaces with the family bedrooms, bathrooms, wardrobes, balconies, and roof terraces are located on the two top floors.

Main staircase in hall with view from living room towards dining room.

Façade towards garden with different volumes and terraces.

Despite these clear divisions Frank succeeded within the central public areas to create one of his most complex and rich interiors. The living room and dining room are on different levels and connected via diagonal vistas. The central staircase and the hall tie together the different parts of this large house.

Movement through the house—"The House as Path and Place"
In his text *The House as Path and Place* from 1931—illustrated with photographs of this villa—Frank describes that we should move through a house just as we move through a city, where narrow alleys lead to open squares that subsequently lead to new, narrower passages. What Frank advocates is variation and dynamics. In the same text he also defines modern architecture with the help of a series of questions: "How does one enter the garden? What does the route look like from the gateway? How does one open the front door? What is the shape of an anteroom? How does one pass the cloakroom from the anteroom to reach the sitting room? [...] There are many questions like these which need to be answered, and the house consists of these elements. This is modern architecture."

The text could be an illustration of how we approach Villa Beer. From the street we move towards the house's large monolithic façade and pass under a projecting element to reach the entrance door. The porch with associated functions such as cloakroom and lavatory announces the entrée into the public areas of the house. The ceiling height on the porch is relatively low at 2.4 m.

After this intimate and complex entrance transition, one enters the high hall, which is the heart of the house, and the central room that connects the adjacent social areas. The room has a ceiling height of 5.1 m. Immediately to the right hand side is a fireplace and built-in seating under the entresol projection. In this part of the room the ceiling height is still 2.4 m. The room-high oriel opposite the entrance door into

View from main staircase towards oriel and garden.

View up through main staircase.

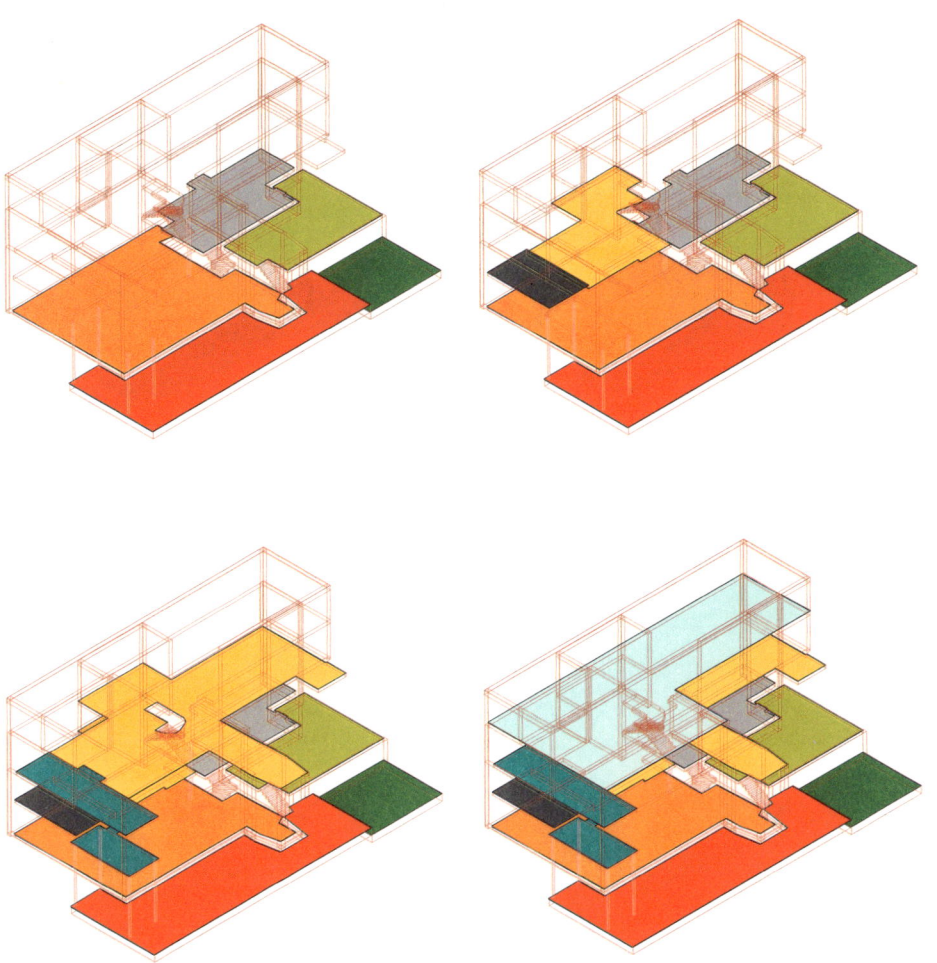

Axonometric perspective showing different levels on terraces outside and floors inside.

View of music room towards tea room with the large round window.

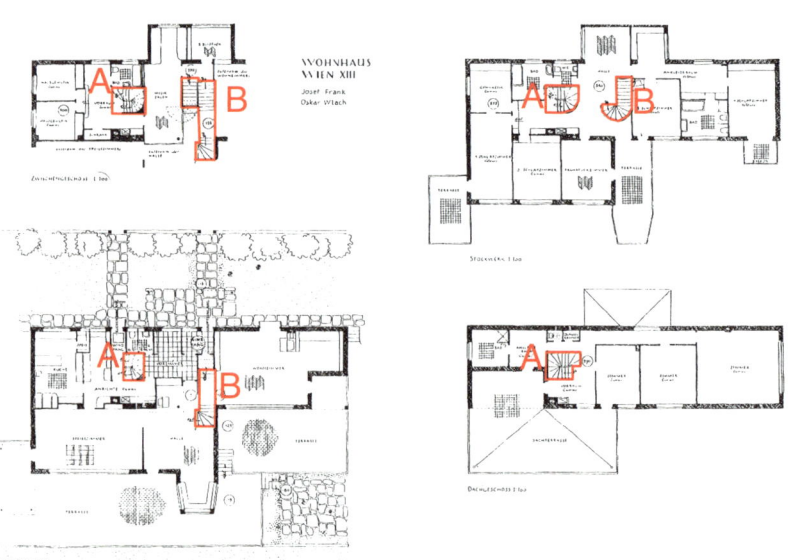

Plans with service staircase A and main staircase B.

Balcony and roof terraces and view of garden side.

Garden side.

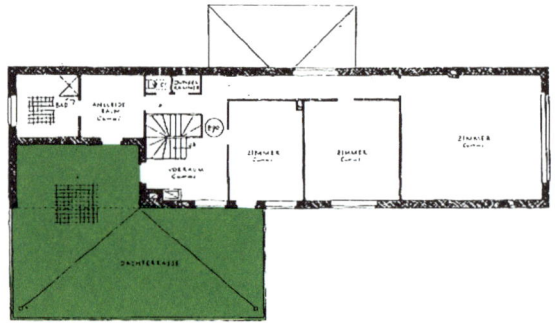
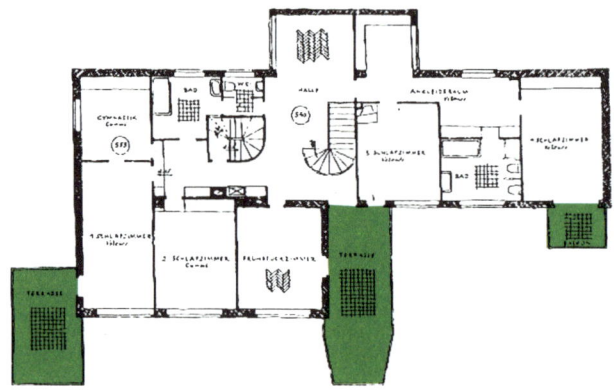
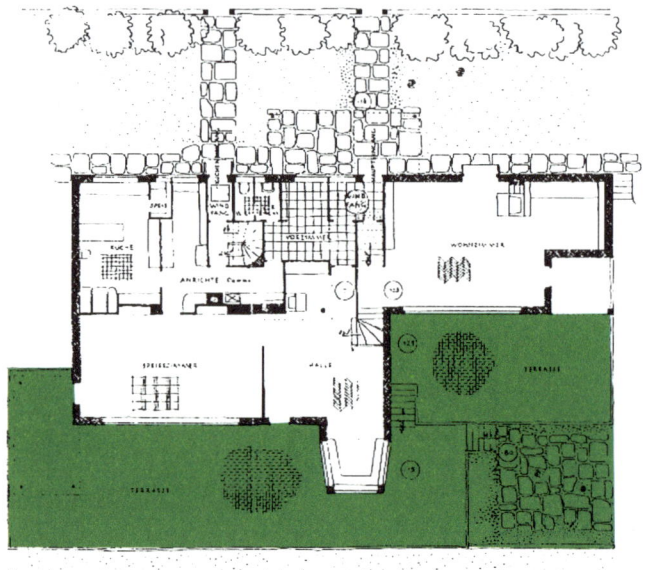

Plans with outside balconies, roof terraces, and terraces in green.

the hall juts out towards the garden and has high windows on all three sides. In a way, the garden outside thus becomes part of the house's architecture and interior.

The dining room on the ground floor and the elevated living room are connected via the hall. The living room's floor level is located at about one meter above the level of the hall. The slender opening between dining room and hall extends almost from floor to ceiling.

Villa Beer is one of the most conclusive examples of how Frank makes use of the Loosian *Raumplan* [spatial plan] that links rooms and spaces at different levels in an intricate spatial puzzle and makes the interior into a kind of architectural landscape. The layout and design of the central hall were presumably inspired by the living halls of English country houses.

From the ground floor a staircase leads up to the entresol which is open towards the hall. Music played on the grand piano on this level suffuses the entire public area. Here the ceiling height is lower, again 2.4 m. Towards the street side, in the so-called tea room, there are two fixed sofas and between them a large round window. The adjoining room is a library with built-in bookshelves. Via an opening in the wall the library is visually connected to the living room beneath.

Stairwells
Villa Beer has two different stair systems. The service stairwell (A) ascends in a rational way through the entire house. The main staircase (B) consists of a system of short flights of steps that together form a molded sequence of events and changes in direction. It starts in the central hall on the ground floor, and after a 90-degree turn and eight steps it reaches the living room level. From here it continues straight up to the entresol (floor 2). By way of a 180-degree turn, the next flight of stairs continues on, ending in another 180-degree turn at the private bedroom floor (floor 3) above. When climbing the

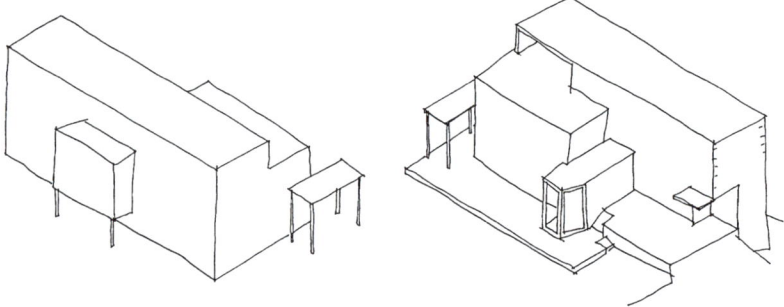

Left volume towards street side and right towards garden side

staircase, one gradually loses sight of the hall and the garden through a diminishing gap between the stairs and the edge of the floor. To proceed to floor 4, one has to take staircase A, to be reached via the common anteroom on floor 3.

Inside—outside
In Villa Beer, as in most other villa projects, Frank is using windows and glazed panels as openings in a monolithic façade. In Frank's architecture, there is neither Le Corbusier's *fenêtre en longueur* with the load-bearing column grid in the body of the house, nor Mies van der Rohe's universal rooms with fully glazed façades.

In Villa Beer a limited number of window types are repeated without any greater dramatization or articulation. The exceptions are the bay windows, the living room and dining room windows towards the garden with their large dimensions, and the large circular window towards the street.

On the elevation drawings Frank shows proportion lines both in the window openings and the various volumes of the building. Recurrent is the classical threefold division of the proportions of both the window openings and the parts of the structure.

Original elevations with proportion diagonal lines.

The house shows a more closed side towards the street and opens up towards the garden. Facing the latter, there are balconies, roof terraces, and terraces in front of the ground floor with few steps leading down to the green. The dining room, hallway, and living room all have large glazed openings with sills towards the garden. There are no door openings in these glazed elements. As a result, the outside appears as if framed like a painting, and it seems as if one cannot move readily between the inside and outside. All three rooms are connected to the outside solely through relatively narrow wooden doors. Just a few years later, in Villa Wehtje, Frank developed the relationship between inside and outside in a more direct and less formal manner.

Higher up in Villa Beer, Frank offers a number of possibilities to step outside. Glazed doors lead to the balcony in front of the northernmost bedroom and from the upper hall onto the roof terrace in the middle of the façade. Two wooden doors open onto this terrace from the second bedroom and from the breakfast room. The third bedroom has a narrow door onto the southern terrace. On the upper bedroom floor there is a large roof terrace, which is accessible via the service stairwell, and a covered loggia, to be reached through another small door.

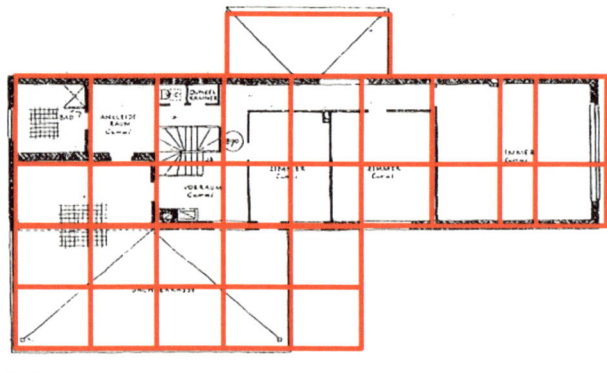

DACHGESCHOSS 1:100

Building volumes
Villa Beer consists of a central rectangular volume of four floors above ground. A central double-high oriel juts out towards the street, supported by two slender, rounded pillars; under this protruding part one finds the main entrance to the house.

Towards the garden the house exhibits a more folded façade with a number of irregular volumes, balconies, terraces, and recesses that transform the rectangular main volume into a dissolved and playful collection of different cubic parts. Variations in the height of the different volumes and balconies create a kind of "landscape" analogy with the garden's greenery and foliage.

Proportions
The house has a strict geometric structure in both plan and façade. The grid has some small variations but consists largely of identical rectangles. Most of the rooms and building elements, both indoors and outdoors, are arranged following this system.

Externally, the façade corresponds to the overall proportions with building elements such as the bay and window openings. Towards the garden, several elements exhibit the classical threefold division.

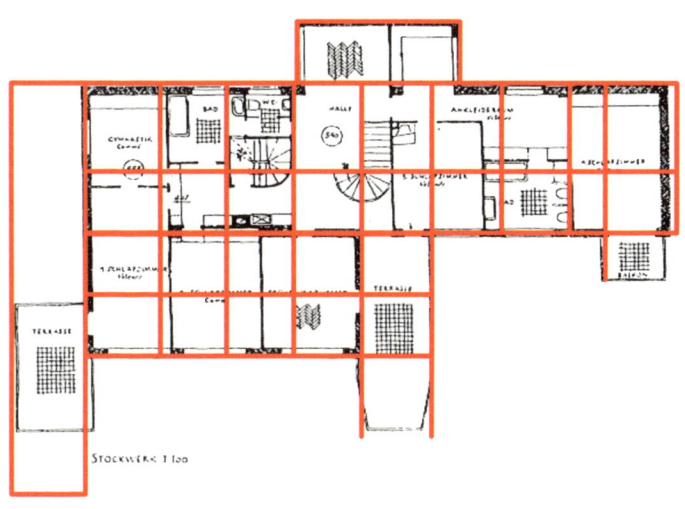

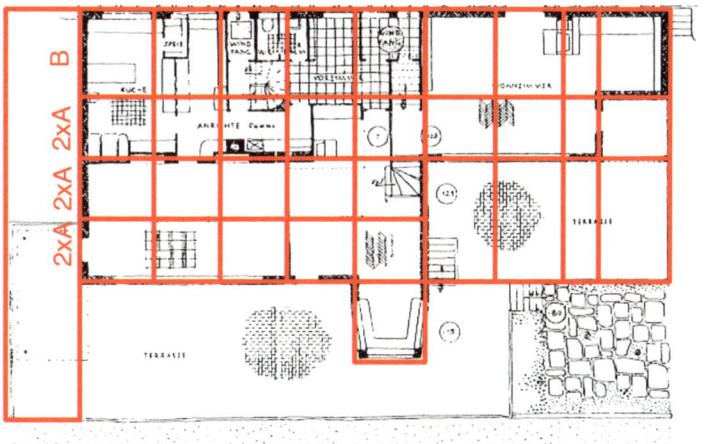

Plans with proportion grid.

Case Study 5

Villa Wehtje Falster 1936

The roof terrace at Villa Wehtje.

View to the western façade.

Case Study 5
Villa Wehtje, Falsterbo, 1936

*Summer house for Walter and Gurli Wehtje,
Rostockervägen 4, Falsterbo*

Of Josef Frank's sketches for house projects in the southern Swedish holiday resort of Falsterbo five summer houses and one extension were realized. Villa Wehtje was the last single-family house to be built according to Frank's design.

The house may, in its irregular form, give the impression of an arbitrary design but is, in fact, deeply rooted in the site conditions. Frank himself describes the project in 1938 in *The Studio Yearbook*: "The house is built on a high, sandy, pine-studded downland, commanding extensive views of the Baltic. The available site was small, hedged in on all sides by other villas – hence the arrangement of the rooms around

View from the roof. Photo from the 1960s.

a secluded central patio, which is lit by electric lanterns set in the outer walls. The roof terrace commands an excellent view over the dunes and sea, and makes for a good dance floor on summer nights (note the open fireplace). This is a summer place, planned to make the most of the short Swedish summer."

Process
Coming to Falsterbo in order to visit Villa Wehtje is a special experience. The house is hard to find, well adapted to the terrain, and today embedded in greenery. The surrounding area is park-like, and the building conveys something slightly informal or unconstrained despite its size. As a visitor, one is not quite sure how to approach it. Originally, the house had striking pink stucco façades.

Villa Wehtje differs in many ways from Frank's earlier realized single-family homes. The main difference is in the shape of the plan and its relationship to the site. At the same

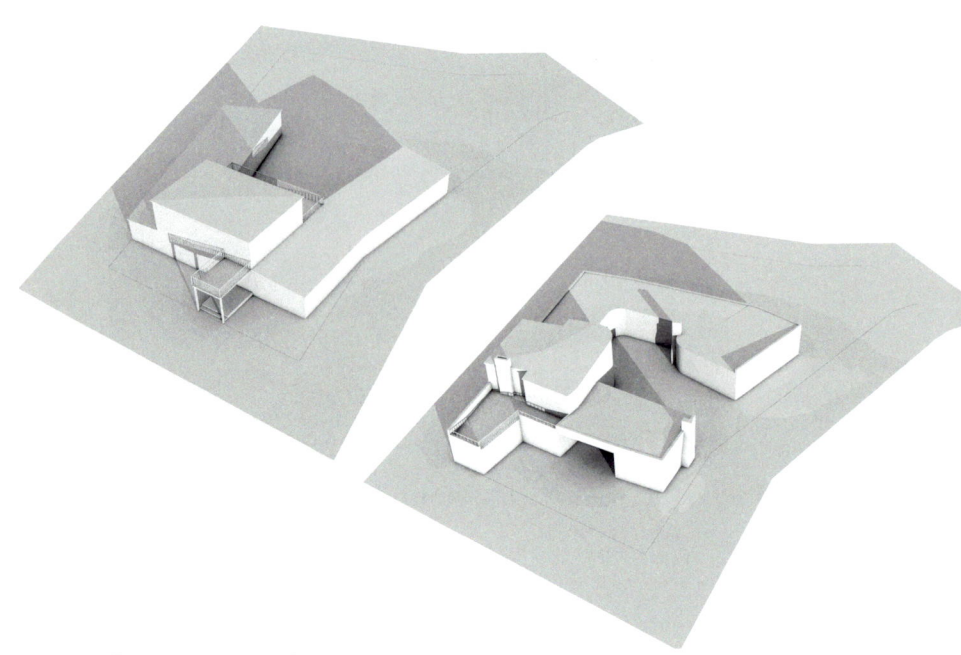

Rendering showing the two main versions on the plot. First version on top. Built version 1936.

time, one recognizes the choice of materials, details, dimensions, and proportions from previous projects. It is also one of the houses that Frank would later in life describe as "really good." Perhaps because he succeeded in combining several of his theories into a built house around the same time that he approached those thoughts on chance and the accidental that he would come to summarize later in life.

As early as 1931, he wrote: "The rectangular living room is the least suited for living in; it is very useful for furniture storage but for nothing else. I believe that if one were to draw a polygon at random, be it with right angles or with obtuse ones, as a plan for a room, it would be much more functional than a regular rectangular one. In the roof ateliers the contingent factors had helped, almost always having an agreeable and impersonal effect."

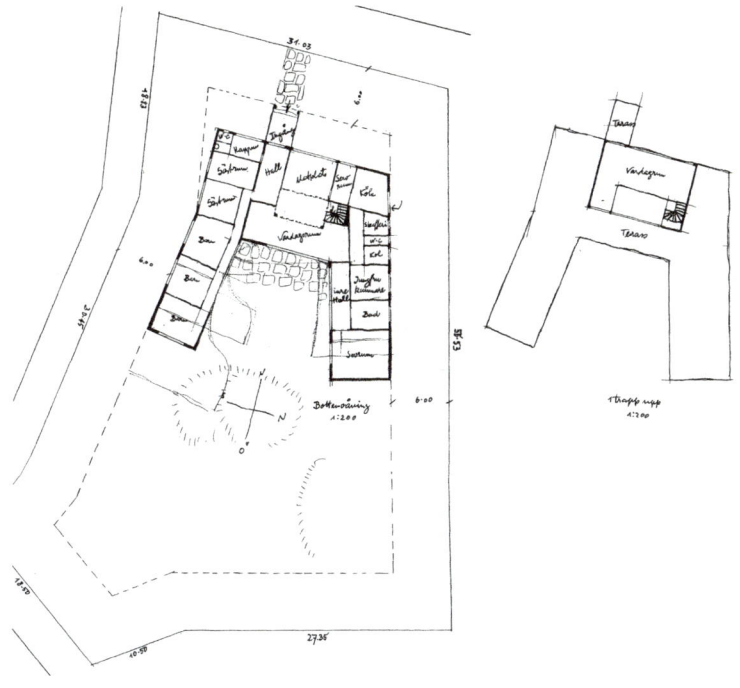

Plans and section of the first version, February 24, 1936.

Plans of the second version, February 25, 1936.

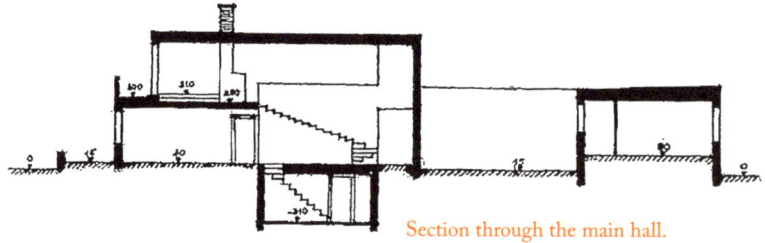
Section through the main hall.

Different versions
Frank produced several dated sketches for the project. Perhaps the most interesting development of the proposal occurs in the second sketch, from February 1936, in which he relocates the house to another part of the site.

At the very beginning, the house had a clear main façade over two floors, an entrance from Rostockervägen to the west, and a courtyard that opens to the east—maybe not the optimal orientation for a summer house in Swedish daylight conditions. The very next day's sketch shows a reworking of the project in which the house is moved slightly away from the road and also turned by 90 degrees, so that the courtyard is directed towards the south, with a terrace to the west. With the house's new positioning, the orientation of the main façade towards Rostockervägen disappears. Instead it becomes a villa with an informal character, somewhat resembling a relatively indefinite grouping of building volumes rather than an integrated and clear structure. The sketches show a house that does not have a clear front or back, non-hierarchical and undogmatic.

Plan principle
Villa Wehtje does not have the same clear principle in the solution of the floor plan as found in, for example, Claëson House. Rather, it is a house that has emerged from the site conditions. Here, Frank came closer to realizing the ideas he developed in his essays of the same time, e.g. *The House as Path and Place* (1931) or *Rooms and Furnishings* (1934).

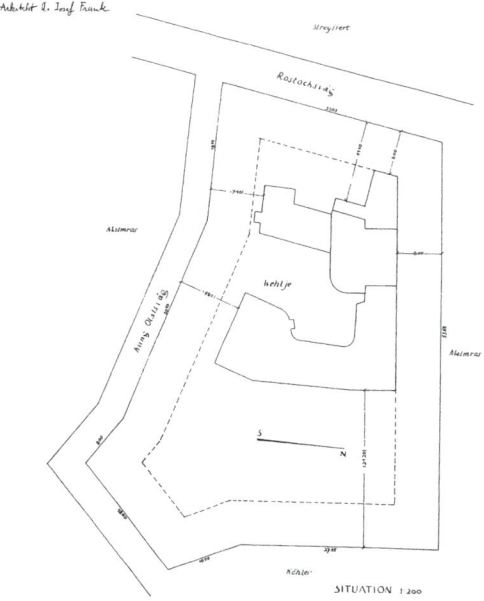

Site plan.

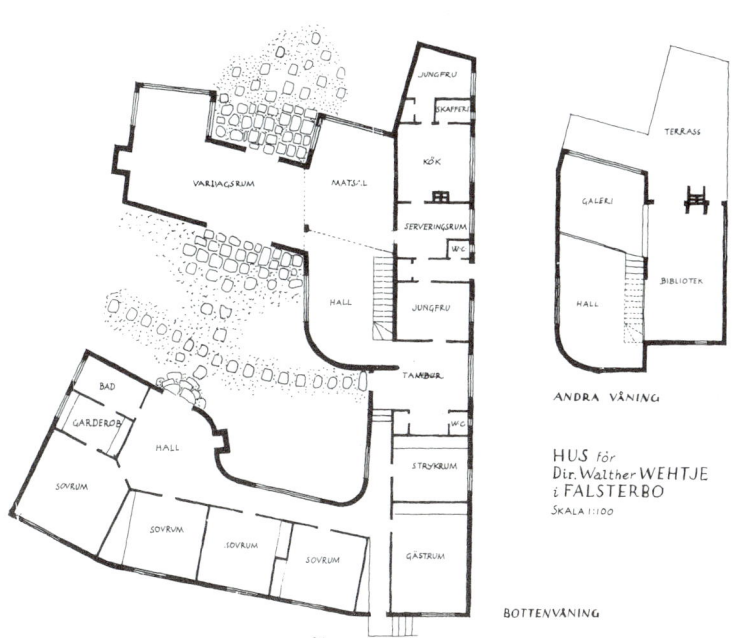

Plans of the built version, 1936.

Pictures of the curved courtyard towards the north.
A part of the room sequence towards the entrance door in the back.

Frank chose to follow the site boundaries for the permitted buildable area and to give the house an irregular plan form. We can call the boundaries an accidental occurrence of the site, which Frank establishes in his underlying idea on room design and his concept of a path through the house.

Villa Wehtje is largely a single-story building, grouped around a courtyard that opens to the south. A smaller part of the house that accommodates the central hall is made up of two floors. Existing buildings on three sides of the property and the requirement to retain two groups of pine trees on the site influenced the shape of the courtyard. Frank, however, created a similar courtyard shape as in earlier projects, such as the first version of House for M S in Los Angeles from 1931.

Room sequences – outside
There is a close relationship between the building's interior and the design of the courtyard. The placingof glazed doors enables free movement between the indoor and outdoor spaces. Outdoors, the focus is on the design of the courtyard's environment, while the ground surrounding the house is left as heathland and relatively undeveloped. The courtyard space is composed of free-formed walkways and random planting.

Well-formed room sequences as part of the architectural experience are a recurrent theme in Frank's projects ever since his previous collaborations with Oskar Strnad and Oskar Wlach. A more or less complex succession of rooms that begins outdoors and continues indoors is intended to create an alternating experience of the house. Among Frank's realized single-family houses, this pattern is perhaps best developed in Villa Beer and Villa Wehtje.

One approaches Villa Wehtje from a small side road that leads to Rostockervägen, from the south between the two courtyard wings. A double-high volume that houses the central hall dominates the serpentine courtyard. In the tall rounded façade sits a large glass panel that helps us find our way deeper

The path continues on the inside. Above: View from entrance hall to the big window and the courtyard. Below: View in the double-height hall, passage to living room under entresol.

View of the living room with the room-dividing pillar supporting the reset entresol.

Approach to the house via courtyard. Room sequences inside on the ground floor and up to the terrace level in the two-story hall. Views from the inside.

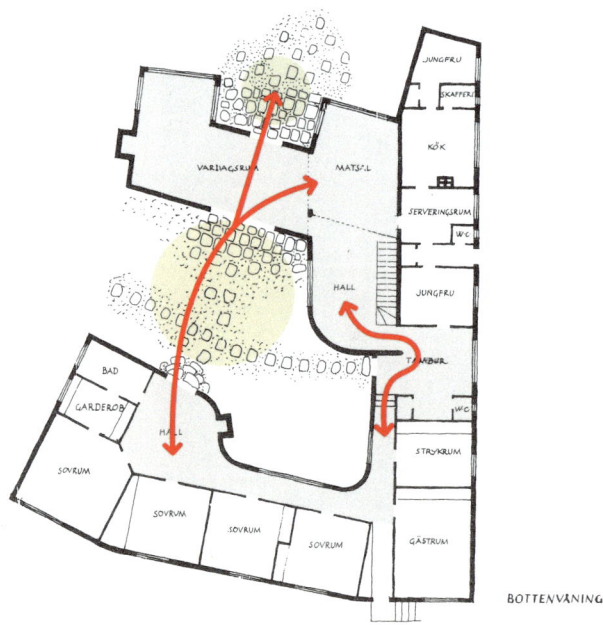

Living room and the hall in the private wing are connected to the courtyard and terrace.

into the courtyard and at the same time offers up a view into the house's heart. The courtyard's elements reveal themselves when moving towards the entrance door, which appears as a discrete, simple entrée at the furthest end of the courtyard, almost hidden by one side of the dominant volume to the left.

Room sequences – inside
Inside the house, Frank works with various ceiling heights, and the contrasting effect between the tall, open courtyard and the entrance hall with its relatively restrained room height is dramatic. A large round window and a check-patterned marble floor dominate the entrance hall. The room is centrally located and separates the public areas from the private bedroom wing. There is a tall, narrow opening that leads into the two-story hall, where the warm southern light shines onto an oak floor through a room-high glass panel — an effective and well-directed transition between outside and inside. On the inside, the movement continues through the public areas of the house in a compound sequence of more or less intimate areas and spaces.

The central hall is designed to provide a visual connection to the upper rooms, but makes us — even though we are given a choice — continue on to the dining area and living room. Both routes in this sequence cannot be perceived in their entirety from the hall.

The hall's double room height accommodates an entresol over the dining area, with two steps separating the upper living area and roof terrace. The entresol floor is, in the meeting between the hall and living room, pulled back from the outer wall and supported by a pillar. This creates an intricate passage between the outer wall and pillar into the living room on one side and establishes a relationship between pillar and dining room on the other side. The pillar thus fulfills multiple purposes, being at once space-generating, functional, and structural element. Its section is not orthogonal but a rhombus or parallelogram, following the non-orthogonal geometry of this intersection in plan on both levels. The pillar has two sharp edges, linking it to the adjacent dining area that can be separated from the hall and the living room by means of two curtains gliding from the top. The two round edges, meanwhile, visually and functionally demarcate the main passage from the hall to the living room and also "organically" allow for "easy access" through this rather narrow passage. As Otto Kapfinger has stated: "The whole philosophy of Frank and much of the essence of this villa is concentrated in this pillar!! What a detail!"

The living room's ceiling height is lower than the hall's but slightly higher than that of the dining area under the gallery. There is a passage between the broad glass panels facing the courtyard and the terrace on the other side. A fireplace and a closed, dark corner can be found in the living room. Daylight falls in from the bright seating area towards the southwest; the windowsills are placed higher up than in the dining room, providing space for furniture underneath. The room sequence from the entrance inward does not run in a straight line, which increases the dynamics and further adds to the spatial experience.

The house's transparency towards the courtyard, through the large glazed panels of the hall and living room, combined with the glass door from the hall in front of the bedrooms contributes to the impression of an integrated room sequence.

Despite the spatial richness in Villa Wehtje, the architecture does not take over but remains in the background. Of vital importance are the rooms themselves and the connections between them, not the salient details, choice of materials or colors.

Public—private
In Villa Wehtje's plan layouts, one recognizes Frank's method of clearly dividing the building functions. Even though the

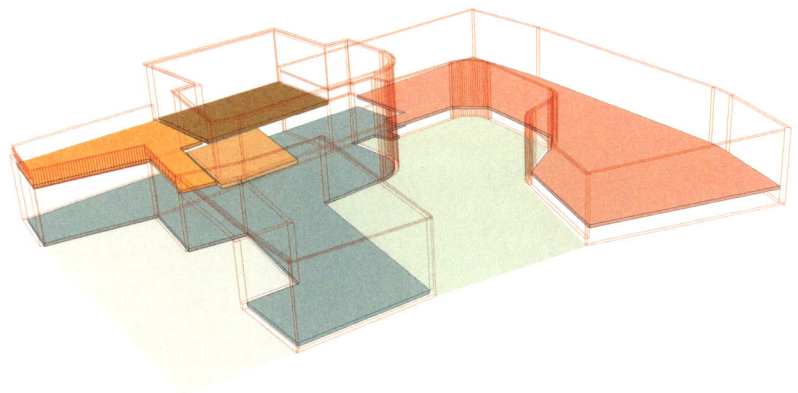

Plans with the five different levels, the courtyard included, in different colors.

Plans with public areas in yellow and private spaces in red, service area in gray.

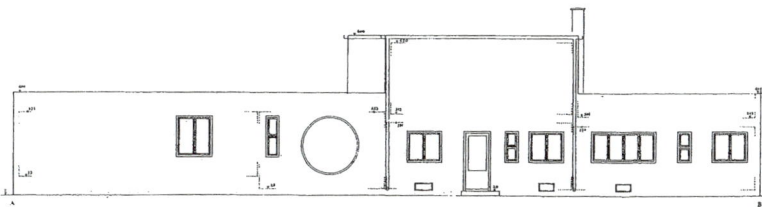

North façade.

View from entrance door to the south.

plan differs from previous houses, the disposition is a repeating pattern.

The public areas are located in the western wing, together with the terrace and courtyard outside, and an upper floor with a library and roof terrace. This part of the house is clearly separated from the service areas, which are situated in the northern part. The bedrooms are on the ground floor but are raised a few steps up and concentrated in the eastern section.

In Villa Wehtje, the serpentine courtyard can be seen as a central space, a continuation or echo of the house's interior. The courtyard is given a background of smooth walls with no recesses into the house.

Volume structure, proportions, and façades
Villa Wehtje has no main façade, and it is difficult to get an overview of the house from one single vantage point. Instead, we see a collection of volumes, which in combination with the silhouette of different roof heights contributes to a diversified external appearance. The double-high hall is a clear and readable part of the courtyard and unites the project into a coherent whole.

Villa Wehtje's façades are dimmed. Despite the pink stucco and the differentiated roof landscape, the appearance of the house makes us think of everyday architecture. The only things that clearly break the pink, plastered surface of the façade, besides the window openings, are the masonry fireplace in visible brick and the reset terrace to the west. The façade surfaces and windows stand in a proportionate relationship to each other, in a way that we recognize from Frank's earlier house designs. However, finding an overall proportioning system for the plan layout is difficult, something that distinguishes Villa Wehtje significantly from Frank's former realizations, for example the nearby Claëson House, which was built ten years earlier. Quite a number of floor plans exist in which Frank grouped spaces around an open courtyard in a similar way as in Villa Wehtje.

Case Study 6

Accide
House
Fantas
House
1947

Renderings of 3-D model.

Watercolor of Accidental House by Frank from the late 1950s.

Case Study 6
Accidental House
Fantasy House no. 9, August 4, 1947

Unbuilt project

Josef Frank made a series of sketches for a single-family house usually referred to as "Thirteen Houses for Dagmar Grill." The proposals, dated between July 22 and August 15, 1947, were sent to her along with comments in seven letters. In the letter that was sent together with Fantasy House no. 9, Frank reminds Ms Grill of his earlier theories and writes: "[…] if you were to draw an irregular shape without reflecting on how it would look as a layout solution, wouldn't this still be a better solution than any carefully planned right-

Letter with D House no. 9, August 4, 1947.

 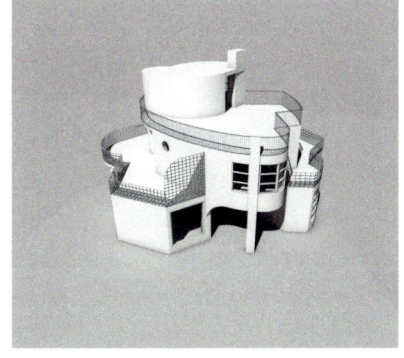

Left: From 1947 with two floors. Right: From late 1950s with three floors.

angled layout produced by some functionalist architect?" Later on Frank compiled the sketches on three sheets for comparison. None of the proposals were realized.

Process
House no. 9 is the most ingenious of the sketches for these thirteen houses—and the project Frank himself was most pleased with. Here he goes one step further, completely abandons the rectangular and orthogonal, and instead creates entirely irregular plans. The house was designated House no. 9 after the numbering used in the compilation of the thirteen letter sketches on the abovementioned three sheets.

After Villa Wehtje was finished in 1936 Frank suffered from no longer having any building projects and wanted to re-engage with architectural projects. The sketches are an attempt to position himself to make a new start, and Dagmar Grill encouraged him to continue working on his designs. The maxim for Frank in these sketches is "complexity" as a positive contrast to postwar architecture's "boring" simplified mass production.

Frank developed the sketches for all of the houses and later drew up these thirteen proposals with plans and façades at a scale of 1:200. House no. 9 can be seen as an exemplary practical application of Frank's postwar theories.

House no. 9 was reworked and refined by Frank with plans on a scale of 1:100 and an elaborate watercolor perspective. In this painting the house is called House for Djursholm. It was also used to illustrate Frank's essay *Accidentism* when it was published in the journal *FORM* in 1958. In *Accidentism* Frank develops his ideas on chance. The text is partly an anti-modernistic manifesto, partly an argument for his intention to create a custom-made house for Dagmar Grill. In the central portion of the text he says: "Every place where one feels comfortable—rooms, streets, and cities—has originated by chance." The picture caption to House for Djursholm reads:

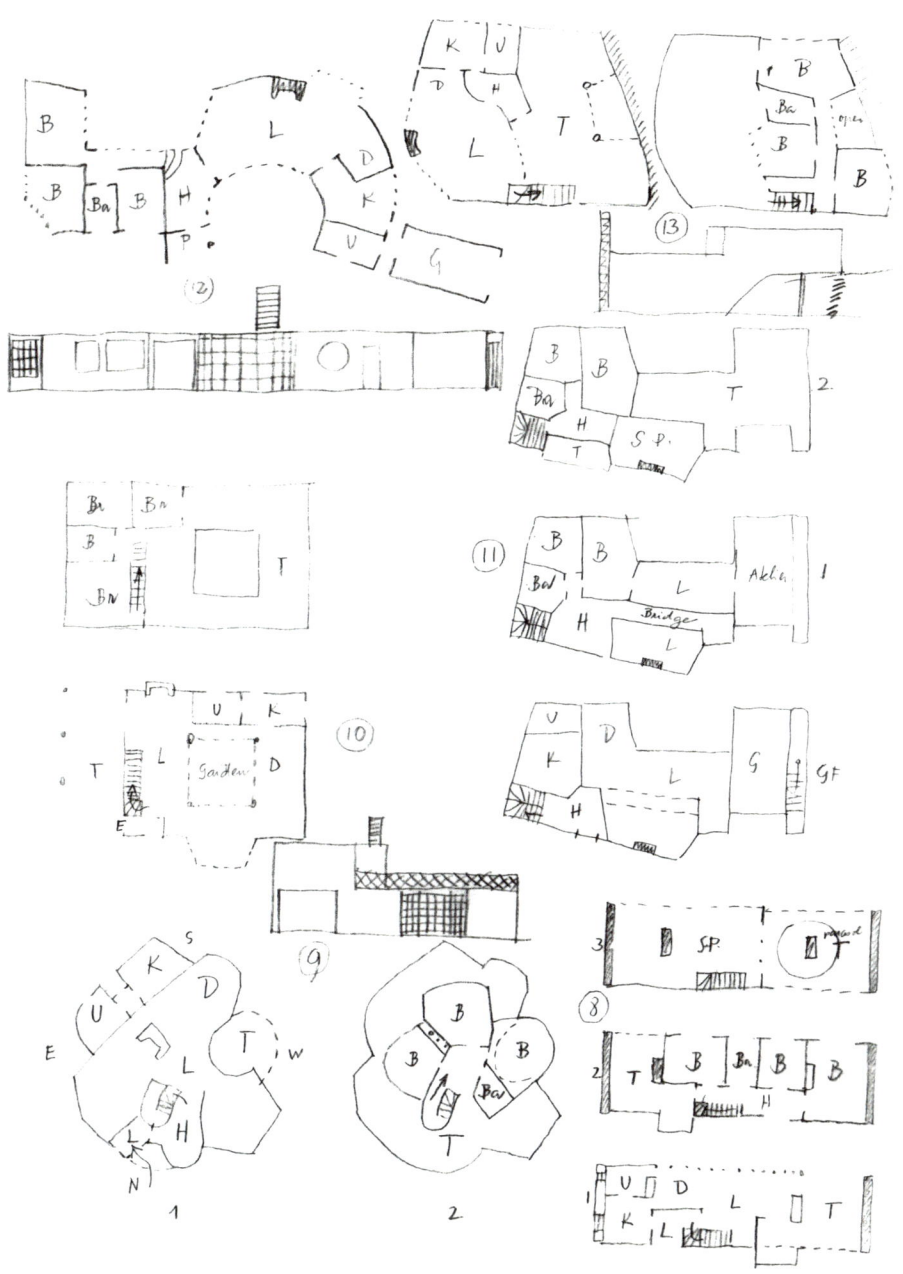

Putting together some of the thirteen D House original letter sketches.

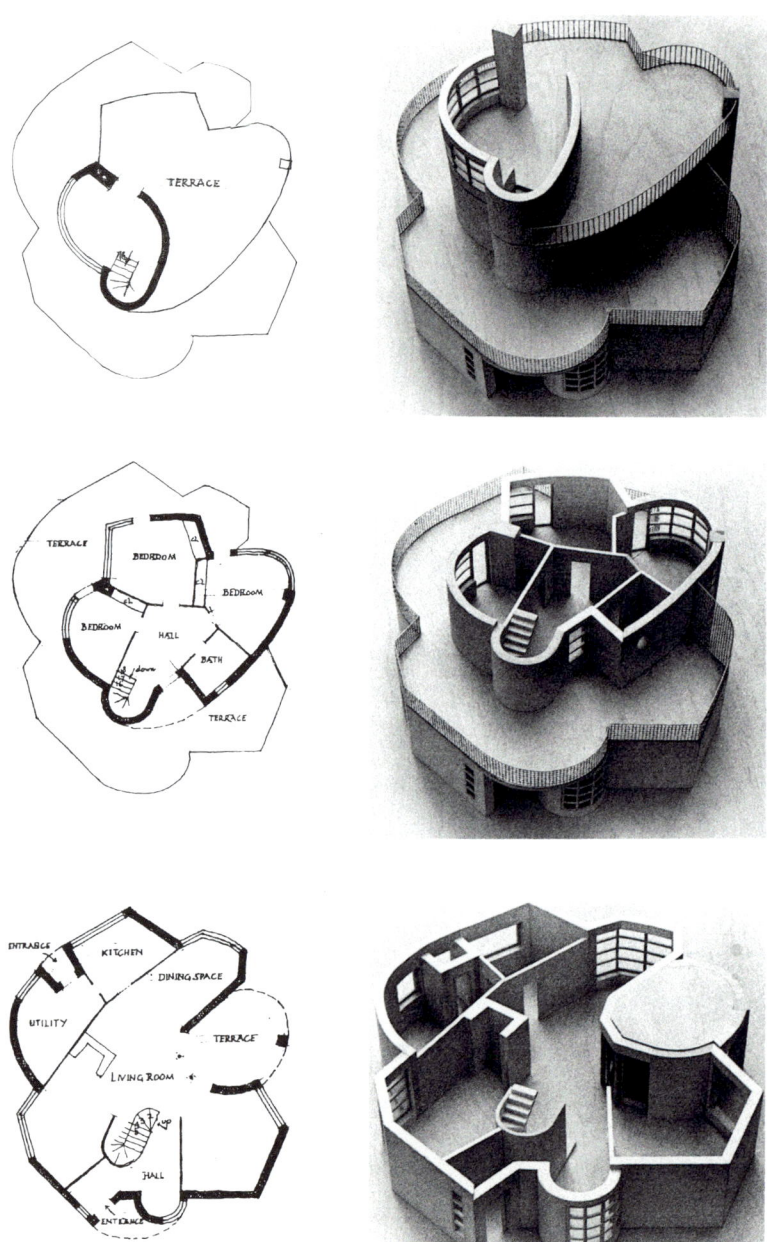

Adapted plans of the three-floor version. For the two first floors, original drawings by Frank; the drawing of the third floor is a reconstruction. Model of the three plans by Spalt/Czech.

"The shape of the house has no relation to its content; in this way one can, according to the author, come to a cozier home than with a functionally planned house." Wether this house was planned for a real plot in Djursholm, an exclusive garden city in the north of Stockholm, we cannot be certain.

With the idea of "accidentism" Frank does not mean to propose arbitrariness or giving free rein to chance but to create as if something had occurred by chance.

House no. 9 is presented in Frank's sketches and drawings as a house over two floors, but in the watercolor perspective a third floor is evident. It shows a penthouse with a roof terrace, as interpreted by Spalt and Czech in the model for the Frank exhibition in Vienna of 1981. Otherwise the different proposals are similar to one another, apart from some variations in the fenestration.

Plan principles
With House no. 9 Frank moves away from the cubic-rectangular plans of the previous "letter sketch" houses. Here he instead draws a plan that consists of completely non-geometric forms that give the impression of being accidental. All the rooms are irregularly formed, which is also reflected in the external design of the structure, both in volume and the façades. These complicated plan forms are augmented by a continuous floor construction with no level changes in the rooms. Despite considerable external differences and an entirely different approach to the room proportions and physical appearance, there are similarities to those house types Frank developed for smaller houses before he migrated to Sweden, for example the Claëson House.

We see recurring themes, e.g. the distribution of functions over the different floors both in plan and section, clarity in the distinction of room functions, the spatial sequence on the ground floor, how rooms unfold as we move through the houses, stair solutions, a compact volume with terraces and an

1.

2.

Approaching the house from the west. Rendered sequence towards the entrance.

3.

4.

inset bedroom floor, close connections between outdoor spaces —the terraces—and the building, etc.

Room sequences and the way into the house
The only information showing the intended relationship of the house to its surroundings is the colorful perspective.

In this perspective a path or some kind of approach is leading to the entrance which is ancillary, almost hidden and not immediately apparent to the visitor. In order to get to the entrance door, we must first pass the lower terrace and go around the house, where we have a look into the center of the house and later into the entrance hall. The entrance door is, as in most of Frank's houses, concealed, protected by the floor of the terrace above.

The entrance and stairs
The entrance situation is a sequence of rooms instead of a clearly defined entrance room as we for example see in Villa Wehtje. The path from the outside and into the house is a swirly sequence of rooms, almost labyrinthine, and continues towards the location where the stair lands in the center of the house.

The formation of the staircase in House no. 9 is an example of Frank's secure hand. The staircase starts at the meeting between the hallway and the living room and is fully visible in the entrance floor's public area. It leads up to the bedroom floor and onwards up to the penthouse and roof terrace.

Light—darkness
Frank believes that part of creating a varied experience within a house is the use of light transmission. House no. 9 has a relatively dark entrance and cloakroom. We are led further towards the light from the small bay window in the hallway, then by the indirect light from the covered terrace. Arriving at the glass panels towards the terrace the house widens and is complemented with direct light from the dining room,

Continued room sequences inside. Entrance hall to the central space just inside the terrace.

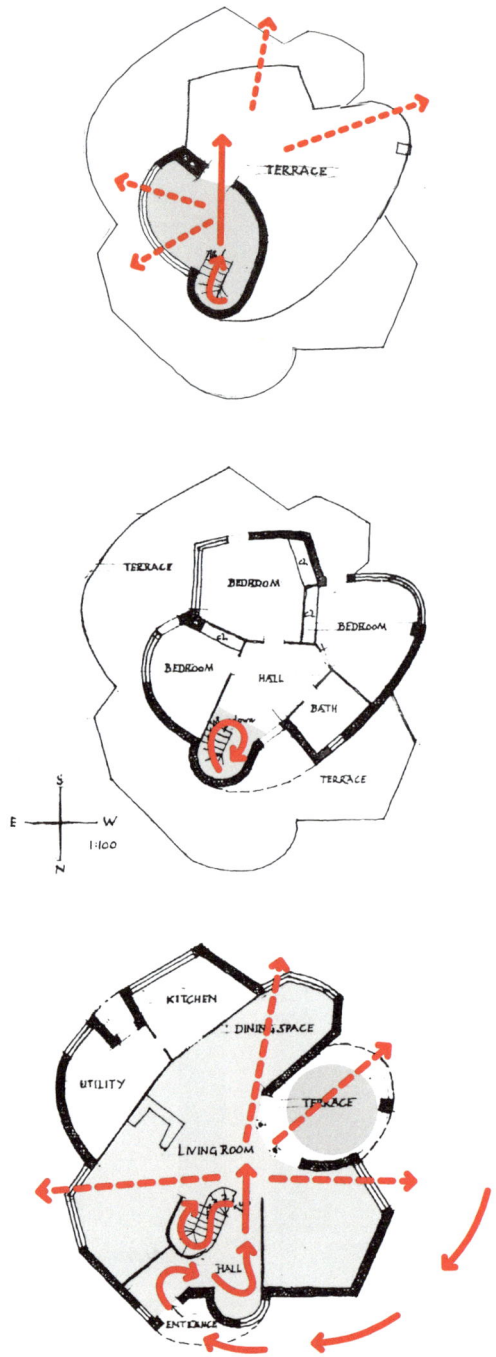

Plans with the path. Views through rooms in dotted red.

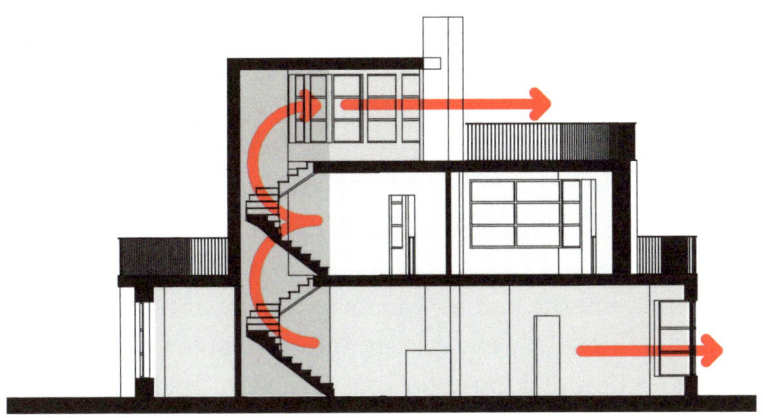

Section. Room sequence from the living area on the ground floor up to the common space on the rooftop terrace. Views.

the living room, and the windows behind the fireplace. The sequence of rooms is characterized by a dynamic incidence of light with closed walls, dark corners, and open window sections.

We do not get an overview of the room sequence until we reach the area inside underneath the terrace. The house's center, or public square, is defined by the fireplace, the staircase and the curved outer wall with its glazed parts. It is an interior landscape with subordinate rooms.

Disposition of the house plans
House no. 9 can, at first glance, seem confusing and complex, but despite the extraordinary plan form, in which none of the rooms have right angles, Frank's distinct way of dividing the house's functions is clearly visible. In his houses with more than one floor he separates living and service areas on the ground floor from a bedroom area on the floor above.

The public area has a continuous ceiling height. The staircase up to the first floor plays a central role within the spatial connection and is located close to the terrace doors in the middle of the house on the ground floor.

The living room and hall have a visual connection to the terrace, while the dining area is in the rounded bay that opens towards the south, turning away from the terrace. Kitchen and service area as well as the cloakroom are separated from the communal areas by door openings or movable screens.

Bedrooms and bathrooms are located upstairs. The three bedrooms and the hall have exits to the upper terrace, which almost continuously extends around the whole floor.

The section of House no. 9 is similar to that of Claëson House, with large public areas on the ground floor connected to the corresponding areas on the penthouse level. In a similar way like in the Claëson House or House no. 3 of the thirteen letter houses, there is a roof terrace at the top. The top floor contains a single room with an exit to the roof terrace looking out to the west.

In House no. 9 the terraces and external spaces are integrated parts of the structure, as in most of Frank's houses. The recess of the ground floor terrace reaches almost to the middle of the house, allowing westerly sun well into the center of the building.

Proportions and façades
In most of Frank's projects proportions and the relationship of dimensions are of great importance. Compared to his earlier projects, there is no clear underlying proportioning system, neither in the plans nor in the façades, apart from the dimensions of the window openings.

It is hard to determine which façade is the main one. House no. 9 appears, if anything, more as an irregular collection of terraced building parts than a clear, well-proportioned monolith.

Structure
In House no. 9 Frank seems to almost completely ignore the static problems that exist in the project. The floor plans of

the house are disengaged from one another and almost arbitrary. Only in a few places are there consistent vertical structural elements such as the staircase, the chimney, or walls that extend from the ground floor to the bedroom floor level. Frank, who was professor for Building Construction at the Vienna School of Applied Arts between 1919 and 1925, postulated that a construction can always be solved technically.

Frank designs windows and terrace balustrades in a conventional manner. He pushes and plays with modernism's limits of material selection. He takes in rural elements like a masonry chimney set against the white façades, which produces a strange, complex mixture of high and low that is bordering on kitsch.

Timeline 1913–57

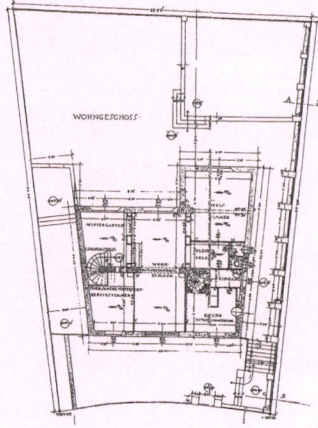
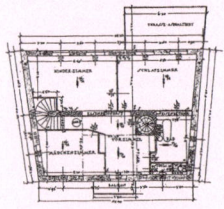
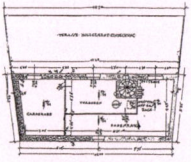

1913–14
Scholl House,
Vienna XVIII

Josef Frank Villas 1913

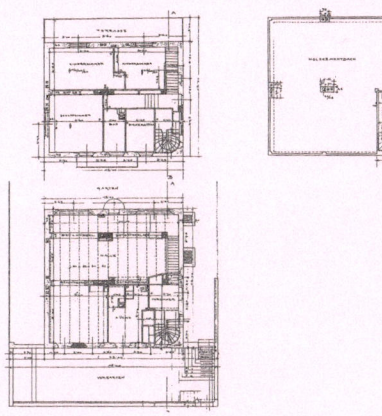

1914
Strauß House,
Vienna XVIII
1925 addition

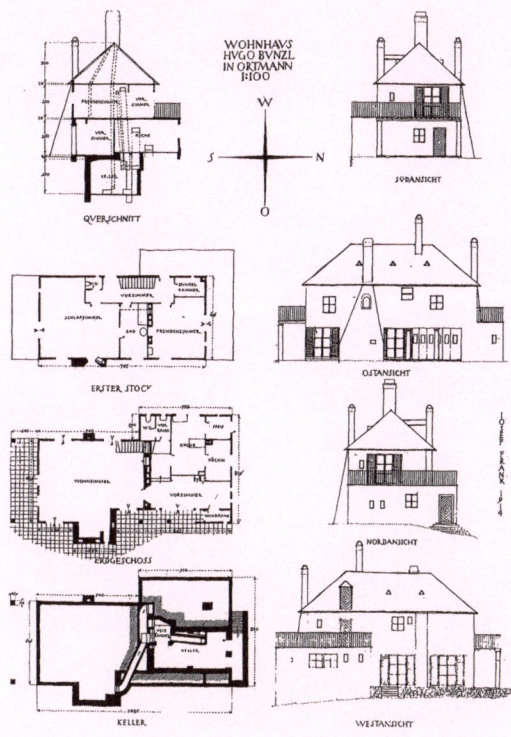

1914
Villa Bunzl, Ortmann,
Lower Austria

1914

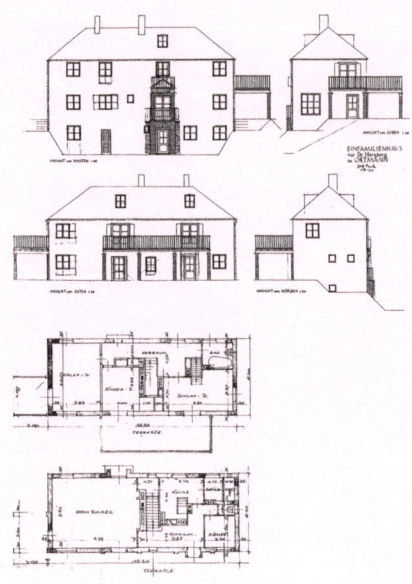

1923–24
Villa Dr. Herzberg, Ortmann,
Lower Austria

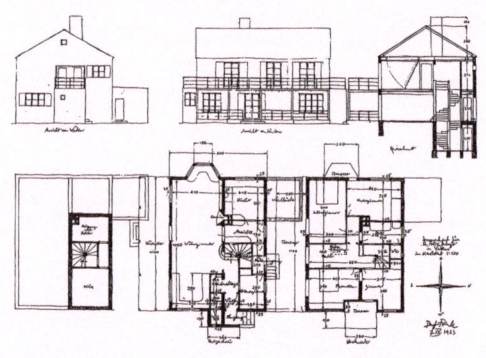

1923–24
Summer House Felix Bunzl,
Wattens, Tyrol, project

1923

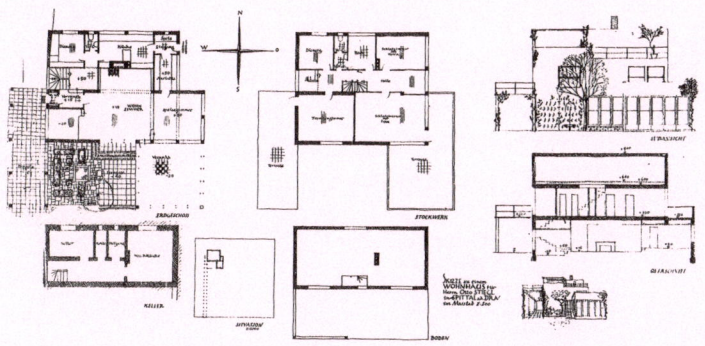

1924–26
House Otto Stiegl,
Spittal/Drau, Carinthia, project

1924

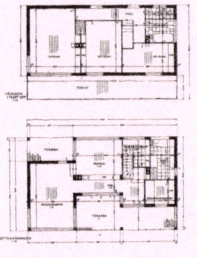

1924–27
Claëson House,
alternative 1

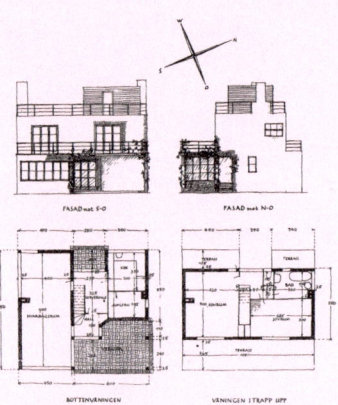

1924–27
Claëson House,
alternative 2

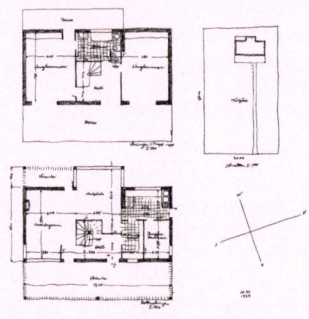

1924–27
Claëson House,
alternative 3

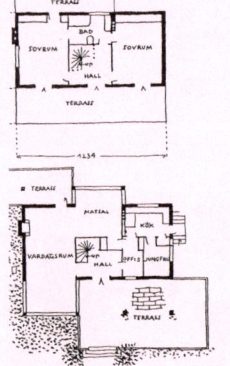

1924–27
Claëson House,
Falsterbo

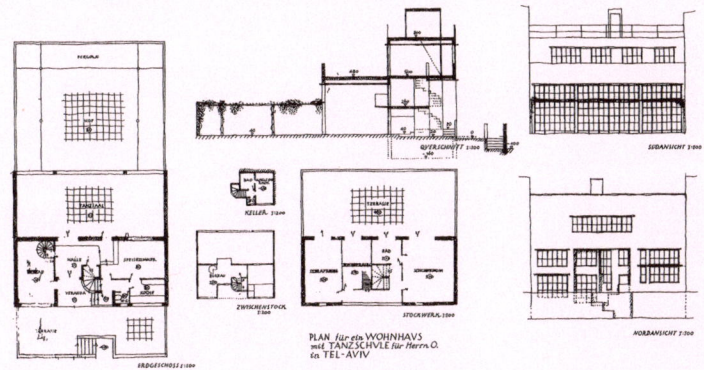

1926
House Dr. Ornstein with Dance School,
Tel Aviv, project

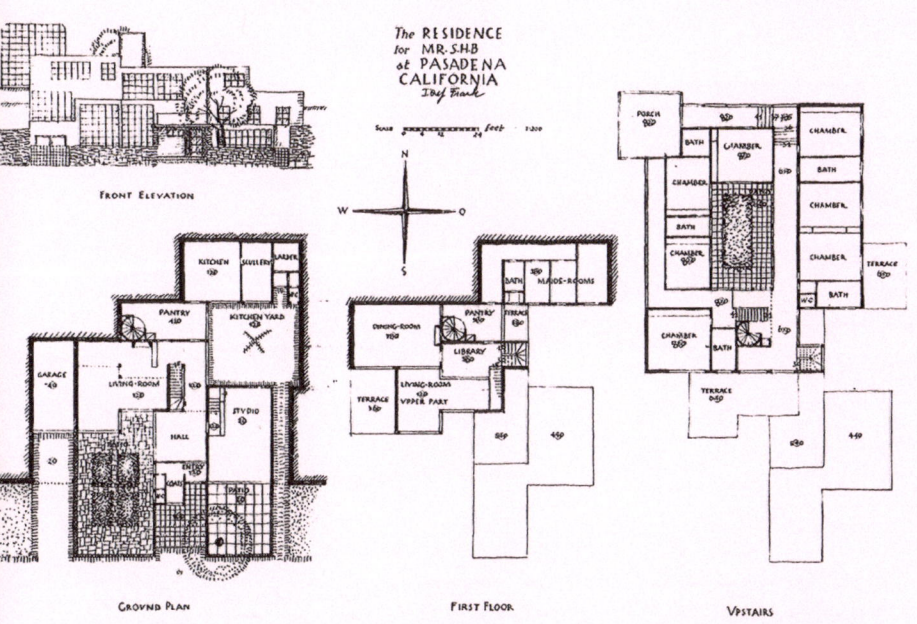

1926
House for Mr. S H B,
Pasadena, Cal., project

1926

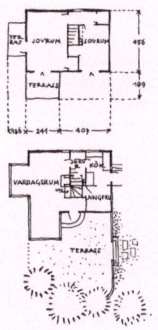

1926–27
House Carlsten,
Falsterbo

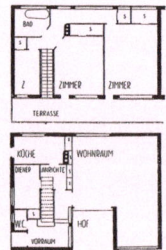

1926–27
Double House,
Werkbundsiedlung Exhibition,
Stuttgart, Weissenhof

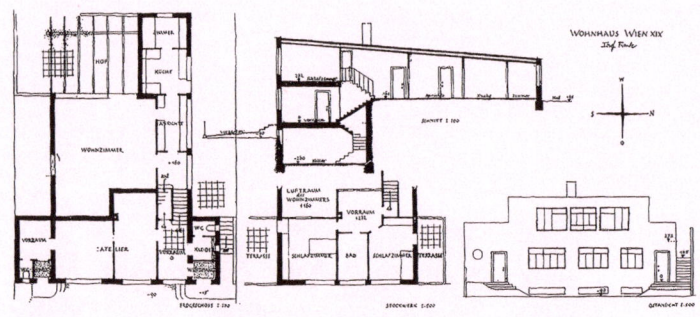

c. 1926
Villa with Shed Roof for Vienna XIX, project

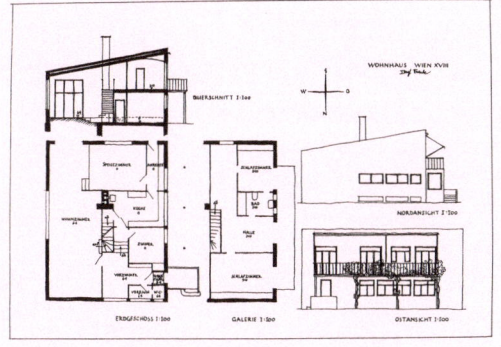

c. 1925
Villa with Shed Roof for
Vienna XVIII, project

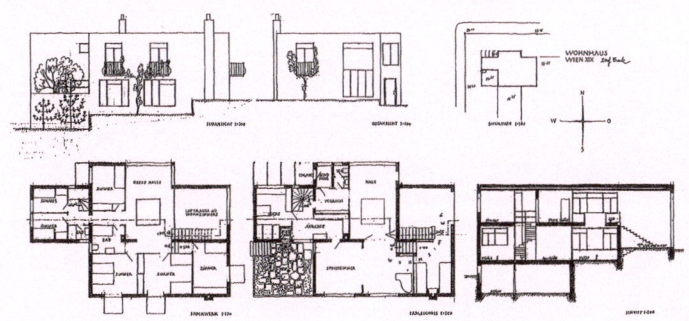

c. 1926
Villa for Vienna XIX, project

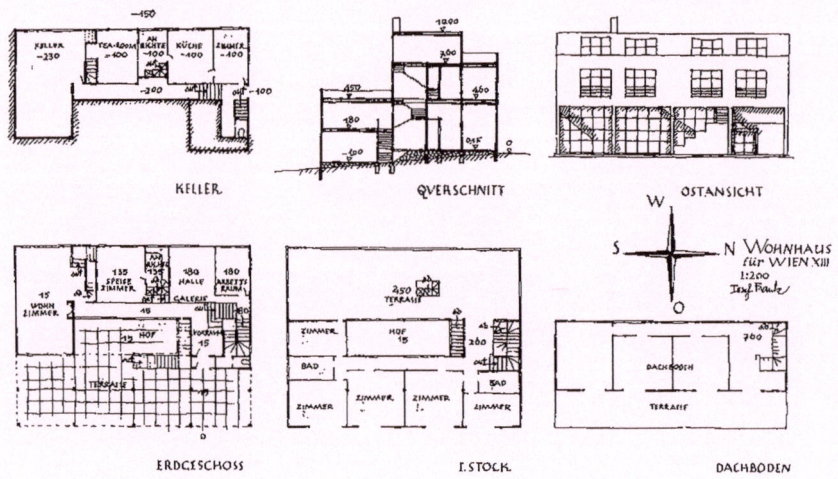

1927
House for Vienna XIII, project

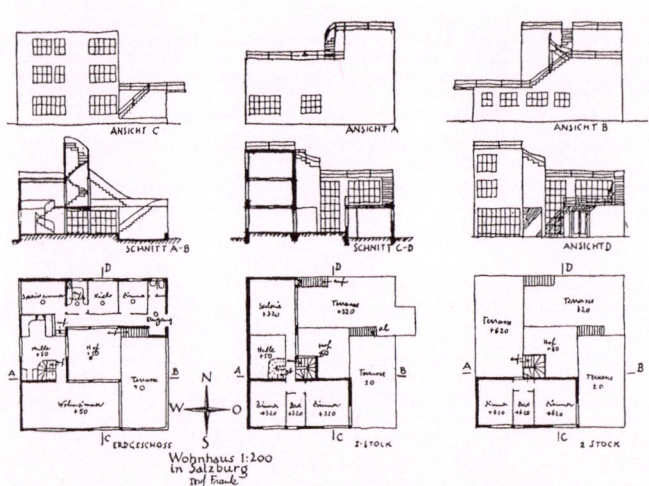

1927
House for Salzburg, project

1927